Christmas 2000

MESSAGES FROM GOD

To Arlene,
May God bless you
richly in the New
Year 2001-

Anne Puryear

Love,
Anne

New Paradigm Press
Scottsdale, Arizona

New Paradigm Press
Scottsdale, Arizona

Copyright © 2000 by Anne Puryear

All rights reserved, including the right to reproduce this book or portions thereof in any form.

For information: address New Paradigm Press,
P.O. Box 12880,
Scottsdale, Arizona 85267-2880

Puryear, Anne
    Messages From God
    ISBN: 0-9634964-4-1
    1. Inspiration   2. Spirituality   3. Religion   4. Spiritual writings

An application to register this book for cataloging has been submitted to the Library of Congress

Anne Puryear
Messages from God
ISBN: 0-9634964-4-1

First paperback printing October 2000

Cover design by Stephanie Schroeder
Cover photos © Bill and Sally Fletcher, used by permission
Front: *Big Dipper in Trees;* Back: *"Bootes & Corona Borealis*
Photos electronically enhanced
Printed in the U.S.A.

ISBN 0-9634964-4-1

This book is dedicated to God,

my Creator

and my friend

TABLE OF CONTENTS

Dedication .... *iii*

Scripture .... *vii*

Introduction .... *ix*

CHAPTER 1

*God explains what it's like to be God and how
he likes to talk with us…* *1*

CHAPTER 2

*God speaks about women, men, children, homosexuality,
abortion, divorce… and clutter* *27*

CHAPTER 3

*Discussions with God about death, suicide, angels,
the afterlife, and souls of animals* *62*

CHAPTER 4

*God talks about telepathy, intuition, dreams,
and communicating with the spirit plane* *97*

CHAPTER 5

*Guidance from God about earthly laws governing health,
weight, and the secrets of staying young* *127*

CHAPTER 6

God on Jesus, Mary, the Bible, prayer, religion and the devil 157

CHAPTER 7

God's revelations on reincarnation, earth changes, prosperity, and healing the planet 195

Acknowledgements 235

Talking with God: A Short History 241

Scriptures, Quotations and Excerpts from Writings about God 246

The Arcturian Connection 261

Information about Logos 262

Order Form 263

About the Author with Photo 265

The Lord God spoke to Moses face to face,
As a man speaketh unto his friend.

Exodus 33:11

MESSAGES FROM GOD

INTRODUCTION

All my life I have had on-going conversations with God. I thought everyone did. I kept journals of my questions and God's answers. When I told my best friend I talked to God and God answered back, she said, "How *dare* you think you can talk with God?" Surprised, I responded, "How dare I *not* talk to God!"

From time to time in years to come, I would cautiously ask people if *they* ever talked to God. Everyone I asked said "no" and many would say, "You can't talk to God," or "You can't talk to God *anymore*." Which meant since the Bible was completed, or since thousands of years ago when the *men* of old talked with Him.

Occasionally I would ask someone and they would say, "No. Can you?" I would answer "Yes, and God answers me back." They would say, "You must have some special kind of gift." I assured them I didn't. I told them they could talk to God too. Everyone would always say, "Oh no, *I* can't. I *pray* to God but He never answers me back." No amount of my talking or sharing my experiences on how I talked with God seemed to convince anyone they could hear God speak too.

So for years I stopped asking anyone. I continued my own conversations with God and wrote down his messages. I felt peaceful and joyful after we talked and our conversations helped me in my life. I always knew what were my own thoughts; but, when God gently moved my thoughts aside and spoke to me, I was often surprised by what he shared.

It seemed somewhat odd that the God I was talking to was so loving and caring about me. He didn't judge me and he seemed to love me no matter what I did or failed to do. When I read the Bible, the God men wrote about seemed so vengeful and angry and condemning. The God I talked with wasn't like that at all. He was comforting and loving and even joked and laughed with me.

I always searched for books about people talking with God, and for writings that would show God to be as he was with me, but I found nothing. As an adult I came upon Eileen Caddy's writings, *Opening Doors Within*, and *God Spoke To Me*, in which she said a voice within, that she called God, spoke to her. When I met Herb, the man who would become my husband, he introduced me to a book he had been given and read daily, *God Calling*. It was written by two women in England who talked with God on a regular basis. These books were the only ones I had read that confirmed what I believed and hoped - that others heard God also. Even with these writings I sensed there was some reticence about claiming it was actually *God* who spoke.

I told Herb that I talked to God and that God answered me back. Surprisingly he not only believed me but also frequently asked me what God said. As I shared my conversations with him, he never doubted my guidance. He told me what a great blessing it was to be able to talk with God and hear God speak. He reminded me that the Scriptures said God talked to Moses as a man talks to a friend. Eventually he began to listen to God speak, also, and has received beautiful and helpful guidance over the years.

Once my youngest granddaughter Krystalyn was spending the night at our home. She was barely three and talked all the time. I was lying beside her trying to get her to go to sleep. I had read her favorite books, made up several stories for her and finally had an idea. I could begin to tell her what I knew about God.

"Do you know that God loves you? " I asked. He's with you all the time."

"All the time?" she asked, sitting up, her long dark hair framing her face.

"All the time, sweetheart. In fact you can talk to God anytime, day or night and he'll answer you back. He loves to talk with us."

"He does?" she asked, her big brown eyes widening. She asked me lots of questions about God and then became very quiet and still.

"Shhh Grandma, be quiet." she whispered, placing her little finger over her lips to silence me. For several moments she closed her eyes and tilted her little head to the side. When she opened her eyes, she put her hand on my shoulder, looked into my eyes and said, "Grandma, God told me to tell you he loves you very very much."

My eyes filled with tears and I held her. This child could hear God too. She lay down and fell asleep in my arms. I said, "Thank you God, for this little soul, and for talking to her."

One day I went to the mailbox and found a package from two women who were friends of my daughter Andrea. They sent me a book and wrote me that they loved it and thought I would too. I looked at the enclosed paperback with a lovely painting on the front. Above the painting was written, *Conversations With God, An Uncommon Dialogue*, and underneath: Book 1, Neale Donald Walsch.

Conversations With God! Someone else could hear God too and had written about it. I was so excited that I sat down immediately and read it during every spare moment I had in the next few days. This writer could hear God just like I did. I was so inspired by the messages and thankful for this man and his courage to share his conversations.

Recently God began to tell me it was time to share my own conversations with him. I had never thought of sharing what we had discussed and the messages I had received. These were private sessions between God and me. It was one thing for God to have others share *their* conversations, but not me. God assured me that there were many things we had talked about, which gave a woman's perspective. He assured me his messages to me would not only help *women*, but also encourage men *and* women to remember it was their birthright to talk with him and hear him speak. He said he wanted to remind them of who they really were, eternal god-beings, his creation.

It's hard to argue with God. As he instructed me, I began to go through what I had received previously, and also began to listen to him daily instead of sporadically as I had through the years. As God and I talked, day after day, and he shared his messages, this book began to take form.

What a gift God has given us, to hear the gentle leadings of his Spirit and let us know how much he loves us. I believe God loves each of us as if we were his only child. Let us together claim from God all the blessings he desires to pour out upon us. And let us, as we listen to the leadings of his Spirit, remember *who we really are.*

These messages from God are the fruits of my many seasons with his Spirit. May they bring you a deeper understanding of his love and the assurance that he wants to talk with you now and forever.

Anne Puryear
Phoenix, Arizona
September 2000

MESSAGES FROM GOD

CHAPTER 1

... God explains what it's like to be God and how he likes to talk with us...

Anne...

Yes, God.

There is something I want you to do for me.

You want me to do something for YOU? Just tell me what.

You and I have talked together since you were a child. As you got older, you wrote down many of my messages to you and saved them. Now I want you to share some of our conversations to help others. I want you to remind my people that I love them and that I speak to each of them all of the time.

But God those messages were for *me and* some of them were very personal. I don't want anyone else to read them. I didn't think when I talked with you over the years that I would be writing and sharing our conversations. It will be hard for me to be open about some of the things I've questioned and labored over.

> Only hard if you make it that way. Only uncomfortable if you worry about what others may think.

I know how much my talks with you have changed my life. I will do what you've asked.

> Good. It's true, some of our talks were personal; but when you go through our daily conversations, I will show you those that will be of help to others. I will help you each step of the way. Many of those who read what I have shared with you will begin to know they can also hear me speak to them and let me help them have a more joyful and productive life.

I will start going through all the messages. I feel better when I'm talking with you every day and asking your guidance about everything.

> Of course you do. That's the way I created you, to talk with me. You can consider me to be your father or your mother, and I can consider you to be my child; but, as our relationship has grown, I hope you consider me to be a friend most of all. For I am the dearest friend you will ever have and you are my dearest friend.

Chapter 1

— ✡ —

I had computer files, several plastic crates, file drawers and many journals filled with my handwritten or typed questions to God and the guidance I had received through the years. I began to go through them and type into my computer those messages that God directed me to share. I also began to listen to God more consistently each day and added some of these messages.

— ✡ —

God, I don't quite understand how you can be with me, and with everyone else all the time too, and know and love each of us the same.

> Anne, you will not understand this fully yet; but as you grow in awareness, it will become clearer and clearer. Remember I told you that in my dimension there is no beginning or end?

Yes.

> The laws, if you will, the energies, the rules, in each dimension vary. My dimension is the combination of all other dimensions, yet is the ultimate state. You could call my dimension "eternity," although that is but a part of it. There are not the same limitations, rules and conditions that you experience in your dimension. Therefore, it is perfectly natural to be able to be everywhere, know everything, and do anything. Even

dimensions that are not this ultimate state have some of these limitless possibilities, but not all of them. In my dimension there are no limitations; yet, we have created in other dimensions many gifts and powers that you would consider miraculous or paranormal. These do not exist in your particular dimension of current existence.

There are many dimensions. Each dimension has limitless and limiting experiences according to the laws and energies governing that dimension. When some expand their consciousness to include both their present dimension and another, they are credited with super-human powers. In fact, it is simply that the limitations of their present dimension are no longer all that they experience.

In your dimension we created women and men and animals of all sorts. Your human life form needs living, growing things to exist healthfully. Many forms in other dimensions do not. Those of you selecting to experience life in your dimension, choose either female or male bodies in order to experience lessons you know you need to learn in order to grow into other dimensions and greater awareness. Sometimes you learn very quickly, and other times you return again and again to learn what must be learned before you take another step homeward.

Another step homeward. You mean back to you, don't you?

Yes. Home. That's why the movie *"ET"* touched so many hearts, *"ET, home!"* triggered memories in so many of you as to where your real home is. By the way, my hand was on that movie; and, if you will see it as so, it is a story of your sojourn here on this planet, your temporary residence.

My hand has been on other movies that some have made, such as *"Cocoon," "Ghost,"* and many others. If you leave the theaters, or from watching the videos, with a sense of hope, of there being more to life, of who you really are, as well as a sense of a greater purpose, then it's easy to see when my hand is on a particular movie.

I felt that way watching the movies with George Burns playing God and a movie called *"Defending Your Life."* Are these other movies that your hand was on?

Yes.

What about movies filled with violence and sex?

When I say that my hand was on certain movies, it means that I sent angels and helpers to work with those developing the movie. The moviemakers were impressed with ways to structure the movie that raised their consciousness and ultimately the consciousness of those who would see their completed work. They could have ignored the guidance I sent to them, but they did not. The movies they created left a spiritual impact on many, including yourself.

Even on movies filled with ugliness and violence I send such a team to help. Usually the guidance is ignored and the completed movie impacts in a detrimental way on those who see it. Have no doubt that such movies harm not help those who see them. They especially do damage to young people as they imprint on their minds and bodies. Children come to tolerate greater and greater violence and often act out much of what they see.

Sexuality in movies is not so detrimental unless it involves violence, such as rape, mutilation, or abuse of various kinds. A movie showing two people who care about each other, making love, is not necessarily harmful. Nor is nudity in a movie shameful. Remember, I created your bodies and minds; and, the human body is beautiful. The act of love can be tender instead of ugly. Often it is portrayed otherwise.

Parents and caretakers should use wisdom in allowing children of certain ages to see particular films. They are not always ready to process correctly what they see; and, everything they see imprints on their minds and bodies in a positive or less positive way. However, for the most part, it is better for them to see naked bodies and acts of love making than the violence in many movies. Ask me about a particular movie and I will tell you if it is wise for you or your children to see it. Safeguarding the minds and bodies of yourself and your young is a sacred trust.

My mother would never let us go to violent or horror movies when we were young. She told us that once something was in our minds, it was very hard to get it out and it was better not to put it in our minds in the first place. It sounds like she was on the right track doesn't it? I remember how frightened I was for days over the first violent movie I saw and couldn't get to sleep at night. Then as a young adult reading a book with graphic violent and sexual situations, being unable to get the pictures of it out of my mind.

Chapter 1

> She *was* on the right track. She prayed for you children constantly, and often listened to me without being aware of it as I sent her ideas in answer to her prayers.

— ✡ —

God, you aren't male, are you? Yet, I think of and hear you mostly as a male.

> No, I am neither male nor female. Yet, because of your religious and childhood programming, you hear me as male. When you are fully integrated you will hear me as both - you will hear the feminine and masculine as one. Right now you hear me as male - yet, you have even told people you sometimes hear a "neutral" voice. That is me integrated in your consciousness as both masculine and feminine.

— ✡ —

If I'm going to share my messages from you, what things do I need to do?

> You need do nothing but believe, listen, write what you hear, and trust, then share. Nothing else. You need not fast, do any special incantations, use any aids, nothing. Just believe we can talk and share together, and in believing let me enter your words.
>
> If along with listening, you will follow a plan that you

feel is ideal for you health-wise, you can stay in greater harmony as we communicate together.

But know this, and tell all: you do not need to be healed to hear me. You do not need to be "saved" to hear me. You do not need to be perfect to hear me. You do not need to do anything but know that I do speak to my children, to my creation. I always have and I always will. That some do not acknowledge it's me, thinking it to be their imagination, or their own thoughts, is of no consequence. I will continue to speak without ceasing until the day comes when you will truly hear and know it is I - your friend, your creator, your God.

God, sometimes it seems so easy to hear you and to feel your presence. At other times I can't even make a contact, or it feels as though I can't.

There is always a contact. You build walls between us. I always hear you. You sometimes think you can't hear me because you feel you aren't deserving, and you have no right to come before me because of your inadequacies. Not so. It is in coming to me that you lose your fears and realize that you are perfection as you are, and that you can make the changes you feel will enable you to be as *you* desire you to be.

Talking with you and listening to you talk to me is like talking to myself. Except, I know what I'm going to say back to myself, and you always surprise me with things you say.

> I am you. I speak in you and through you, yet I am also outside of you.

God, I need your special help and blessings to do this.

> Anne, I bless you with each breath you take and with each thought that comes to you. Come; let us create together. Let us create this book and share my messages to you. For you and others are to be Awakeners.

What a nice word. Awakeners.

— ✡ —

God, I fall so far short and I am so lacking in discipline. Many others are better prepared and more spiritual. I'm not asking for praise but to understand. Why me?

> Some praise does not hurt. But, it is your very question that allows you to hear clearly; and, you have a pure heart. That counts for something - a pure heart - and you have that. Plus you have listened to me most of your life and trusted in my guidance.
>
> Because of Neale Walsch, and his courage to get the guidance I gave him out to the world, thousands of people will begin to listen to me again. Many, like yourself, will also have the courage to share with others what they have received. Then a great and mar-

velous thing begins to happen. My messages and your words spread like wildfire. A massive movement in consciousness is crucial in order to help restore the planet and its inhabitants for this time and for the future.

Many books will be written - some will call them copycat books. In truth, any books of my messages are not "copycat" books, but different perspectives of my guidance. Many will be sincere and from the heart and those who read them will know of the truth they contain. Some will be written from ego and not from listening to me. Far more will be a sharing of our moments together. I would that there were thousands of such.

Because of the mother you chose, you were instilled with a love of me and of yourself as my child. You were taught that I am a loving, not a vengeful, God. Therefore, communication with you was easier, and was a joy because you trusted me and loved me. I didn't have to break down as many barriers as we talked together.

But God there are books by others who have listened to you. Is this book really needed?

Does the world need another book about my messages - a resounding *YES, YES, and YES!* It needs a thousand books because no one person, no hundred people can begin to cover all I desire to say to my beloved ones. Each perspective of my messages helps others. That is, the very communication which is filtered through your own consciousness is of greater help to certain individuals, who, perhaps, could not so easily understand the messages of another.

Now, let me more fully address "filtered through your own consciousness" since that is a stumbling block both to you and to many others. Without your early childhood programming, you would respond to me in a different way; and, I would be limited in what I could impress you to listen to and to bring through. Your higher self and my spirit are in rapport at all times, as is true for all. Therefore, when I impress on your higher consciousness a particular truth, it is nurtured as it enters, by your perceptions of things. It is honed so to speak into understandable verbiage that enables you to comprehend what I wish to make known, and thus enables you to put my messages into helpful and hopeful dialogue that others can understand.

You have a greater understanding of my communication to you, because it comes directly through you and is only altered slightly by your own perception. Those who read what you write may perceive slightly less fully and those they then share this with even less fully. This is why everyone should listen directly to me for the fullest personal understanding for himself or herself.

God, how can others and I stay on the right pathway without ego and pride?

Anne, you know the answer to that.

I do?

Yes.

Well God somehow at this moment I am not all that clear about the answer. Could you just tell me again or help me understand better?

You can help others more and be more successful by setting the goal of what *you* really want to do with your life, not what others want you to do. There is no ego or pride in that. It is your birthright to accomplish whatever you desire to do with your life. When you *know* that, there is no pride, and there is no humility. There is the claiming of your birthright in my name.

If you do a work that you have chosen and love, you will want to share what you learn with others. You will prosper in all the ways that are important to you. Ego and pride come from lack of self love and feeling you are not doing what you really want to and what would bring you joy in your life.

All the things you desire and more I gladly give you. I do not want any of you to suffer nor to be tested nor to want. I desire you to have whatever good things you desire. I gladly give them all to you. Just believe what you have asked for is yours, lean to me for understanding and take every opportunity to share what you have learned with others. There will be no ego or pride when you do this.

Chapter 1

> Listen to me more often and know this - you are loved. All of you are loved. You truly are a soul having a physical experience, not a body having a physical experience. You have always been and will always be. And, this incarnation isn't all that bad for you. There have been worse, many times worse. This one is relatively easy, as you have sometimes known.

Yes, I have felt that despite some difficulties this has been a very good life.

> I created you and every soul to have joy - claim that. I know you as no one else does. I created you to become better through this very experience. I created you to love and to be loved. Yes, people you love have hurt you, and sometimes you have hurt others. You have rarely hurt others intentionally, but others sometimes *do* hurt you and each other *intentionally*.

> You do have a pure heart. Yet, when I tell you that, you doubt it's me. A pure heart is just one that doesn't find joy in being mean, doesn't hurt intentionally and wants to make the world a better place. You then, by *my* definition, have a pure heart. If you look around you will discover that there are a great many of you with pure hearts.

Telling me I had a pure heart made me doubt it was you because I knew what unloving thoughts I sometimes have. This explanation I can accept. I do know many people who seem to have a pure heart.

> Count your blessings and then begin to create a pathway that will bring you joy and enable you to make

the most of each day, each year. See, it's that simple. Find what brings you joy and make the most of each day. That's my great truth.

Don't seek world fame. Seek my guidance, and whatever you want will come to you. When you love yourself, you don't need the world to tell you how great you are. And, you don't need to tell the world how great you are. It is enough that *WE* know. And, when you finally learn to love yourself as I love you, healing is deep, and growth occurs. Pride and ego vanish.

You want to write - then *write* - hourly, daily, not feeling isolated, for you always have me for company. Then you will write more and more and speak more and more to help bring heaven upon earth. You will help heal the awful wounds and scars humankind has about their understanding of me; and you can heal the deep wounds and scars that women have about me as a male God. Others have *different* missions they want to accomplish. They must set themselves to it. Begin it now. Never give up. All of you are needed to bring heaven upon earth again.

Then help all of us.

Anne, I always do.

Chapter 1

God, I *do* love you.

> Bless you my child for I love you all there is. I love you as if you were my only child. You know what I mean by that - that I love you as if there was only you in all my creation.

I love it when you say you love me like that. I feel sick when you say you love Hitler the same although I try to understand it.

> But, you know it's true.

Yes, but it is *really* hard to understand.

> You don't remember, yet, but you know that no soul can be lost – *ever*. There is nothing any of you can ever do that keeps me from loving you and patiently waiting until you find your way back to me. If you can't do that yet, I will embrace you with my love until you wake up and begin to remember who you are and that we are *one*. Some souls may not turn their lives to the light nor find themselves this lifetime, or on this planet; but I will seek them out throughout the eternities. None can be lost to themselves or to me. For some of you it may take a lifetime, for some milleniums of lifetimes. I will wait. For you cannot be lost to me.

> Did I not send you this message in the parable of the prodigal son who returned and was welcomed by his father, and in the parable of the ninety and nine sheep left in the fold, while the Good Shepherd went back to find the one still lost? This promise to all of you is not hidden if you will seek it out. Rather some teach-

ings would have you believe that I would desert you because of the unwise choices you make that slow your growth. In your soul you know better than that. For I have loved you with an everlasting love, and underneath you always are my everlasting arms. Always. I will wait for you forever. I will seek you unto the ends of the universes. If you think you cannot find me, it is not I who have moved away. There is no place you can go where I am not.

What would you ask of me Anne? For I want to answer every question of your heart?

I want to understand how to live a life that is in balance and harmony.

You do understand it; but you must *apply* what you know. Taking care of this sacred temple, your body, is important to help you house your soul for the optimum length of time to learn all you can, to do all you can and to have all the joy you can. I will talk with you later about eating living foods to maintain your spirit.

And, you must love if you want a life of balance and harmony. You must love everyone, even when people deliberately lie about you and hurt you. Even when things don't go the way you want. Love is really all that survives, that means anything. You must love so fully it overflows. Give yourself away in love. Heal yourself with love.

> If you would listen to me, even for a few minutes, and record daily what I share, you would enable me to help others. I would also be able to help you more fully if you would come and talk with me more often. Every time you desire to change, it's easy. It is only hard if you try to do it all yourself and forget that I can help you. I don't want you to be unhappy or to fail at what you love. I want you to be so filled with joy that you want to wake up dancing, and to fall asleep laughing. I want this for you and for all of my creation.

I love the things you say. I do have another question. What does the scripture, "Ye are gods, children of the most high," mean?

> I am God. You are not God, but you are gods, children of the most high, my creation and my co-creators. We are one. Remember I told you that I am in and through you but I am also outside you? While you are in the earth form it is such.
>
> The secret of happiness is knowing you are gods in the making. You did not originate on the earth and you will not stay here. Indeed you are being prepared to aid in creation elsewhere. Therefore, consider your sojourns here to be great opportunities for growth and joy. For one day all will be one with me and there will be no more death and no more sorrow.
>
> The material world holds and controls most of you. Things that will pass and be dust have become your gods. Souls that will never perish are neglected.
>
> Joy, which is your birthright, is lost in worry and fear. You forget who runs this universe. You are gods, chil-

dren of the most high, my beloved ones. Let nothing become your gods and keep you from this soul evolvement.

Today you learned lessons that defined who you are and what you will become by how you handle them. Ask empowering questions that help you grow. Listen and you will receive empowering answers. Do not ask questions that cause your mind to tell you what a failure you are or that you cannot do something. Ask me questions that will empower you as I answer.

This is a time of great growth for you and for others who put me and their spiritual growth first and follow my light. Let me direct you. Hold only love in your heart. Be not broken by the winds of change. Bend with them.

Welcome the winds and let them make you strong. For I will still the winds when needed.

When you sometimes feel irritable or agitated after talking with me, it's because you feel you have left my presence and you want to return. You haven't left, and I never leave you. You can hide in all your busy-ness, but I'm still with you. Become more aware of me in every moment of your life and with each breath that you take and you will know that I am always with you.

Chapter 1

Good morning, Anne.

Good morning, God. What message do you have for me today?

I am you. You are me. I am everyone. You are everyone. Everyone is us. There are no *they and we*. There is only *one*. Such a simple truth – most make it difficult.

It sounds good, God; but it really is hard to live. Help me feel that oneness so that you can speak to me more easily and I can receive your guidance more accurately.

Their own feelings or perceptions of course, color some of what everyone receives. So, you must sort out what is your truth and what isn't as you listen to any guidance. For instance, you have had some concerns at times about this book and your own feelings. Some things you felt to be correct, others were not what you had previously believed. As you worked with these feelings, you allowed yourself to expand your consciousness.

While it is true that I as your creator know that the ultimate outcome of each soul is certain, it is wrong that I don't care what one does. Of course I care, because I see needless suffering because of incorrect choices, or delaying choices.

So, I God *do* care, and this is very important, because it is deeply discouraging to feel I am so unlinked from humankind. I care deeply; but I do not get discouraged or hopeless or give up on you, as most of you do with yourselves, when your choices take you off the

> track for days or years. This is because I do know the ultimate outcome - one day you will come home to me. It may be in a moment, it may be in several lifetimes; but, the outcome is certain - we are all one and one day you will remember that.
>
> What you do to help one helps all, especially yourself. What you do to hurt one hurts all, especially yourself, because we are all one.

Sitting by the lake one sunny afternoon after canoeing, I wrote in my journal, "God, I'm discouraged."

> Yes, I know. What a wasted place to be in. It is my good pleasure to give you the keys to the kingdom - you don't even reach for them. What a sad state of affairs. You and most of the world. So few get done what they came to do because they let discouragement take over.

The keys to the kingdom! I don't know what that means; but, it sounds good.

> It means I can give you the keys, gifts, the ways to unlock all the doors that are keeping you from all your blessings and good. It means to give you everything I have, everything you choose. Let me know when you will so allow it.
>
> When you are discouraged, claim without hesitation

or reservation all your blessings. You can see, you can breathe, you have people who love you and people you love, you have food to eat and a home. You can talk with me. What is there to be discouraged about? You are co-creating with me. Every thought is a creation of good or ill. Every action is a creation of love or of fear.

Create only love and you and your planet will grow well. Create fear and discouragement and the planet shrivels. I am here at this lake with you, but I am everywhere. You feel me more clearly here because of the peace and stillness and the sounds of my creation. But, I am in the chaos as well. It is just harder to sense me. Many of those in physical bodies slumber. They need awakening. We will reawaken my children.

Also, Anne, you have always been too hard on yourself, since you were a child.

Were you with me then? Of course you were. I just realized you *really* know me. You're the only one that knows my whole history. You watched me grow up as a baby, a teenager, married, divorced, married. You have seen and been with me through it all haven't you?

I have. Every moment of every day of every year, watching you, loving you, encouraging you, understanding you, waiting for you to hear me better. Now you hear me much better; and, it's been worth waiting for. You are one of the ones who is going to help remind the people of your generation, your world, your dimension, your time period, to know me in a different way. To know me in the way that I truly am - filled with love for you, for each of you.

> You must have no jealousy of my love for anyone else. It is impossible for me to love anyone more than I love you. It is impossible for me to be prouder of any creation more than I am of you. That is what being God means. In my dimension the rules are such. I truly do love you as if I had no other children, as if you were my only child. I can't say this often enough.

That makes me cry God. I know that I've always felt your presence and your love; but I didn't always know what I was feeling. Now, I have begun to remember your love from all those years.

God, help me understand more about death. My mother just died and I love her and miss her. She was a really good mother and always made us feel loved. She loved us like you do, as if my brother, sister and I were each her only child.

> Picture your mother being held in the palm of my hand. Now, picture yourself held in the palm of my other hand. This is death, being lifted from one palm to the other, yet always connected. I hold you both. You just rest in different palms for a moment. Now I hold both your mother and your son Stephen in one palm, you in another. You are still one with me and with each other.

That's comforting, because standing on one palm I can yell across to someone on the other side. They can hear me, and they can call back to me.

> Yes, they can hear you, and often you can hear them. There is no death, as such, only the change of form from denser physical to lighter spiritual. The soul never dies, it simply continues in this different form. By raising your spiritual awareness through dreams, meditation and moments of quiet, you can often attune to the souls of those you consider dead.
>
> The love and caring you have for those in the spirit plane and the love they have for you does not die or lessen. It grows. When you sleep and the lighter spiritual body lifts from the denser physical form, you play together, and talk together as you did when both of you had physical bodies. When you awaken, you often forget that you were together. The pain of seeming separation is only because you don't consciously remember these visits.
>
> You will live forever with me. Your form will change, your consciousness will change; but you will live forever. You and all those you love, all you have loved and all those you will ever love.

That's great.

God, how is it that when I ask to speak to someone who has died, or to one of my spiritual helpers or angels, I feel the need to pray and surround myself with light and protect myself? Yet, when I speak with you, I feel no need to do any of these things. I *know* you're there and that I am totally protected.

Your soul knows. Your soul is one with me. It's that simple. You know that when you ask to speak with me, there is no need for such protection. I have always been with you, from the beginning to the end of the circle of life and throughout eternity. Of course the circle actually has no end or beginning, as is true with your soul. We have known each other forever.

Others that I send in my stead, angels, guardians, guides do not have such a long history with you. Because so many in those dimensions desire to speak, it is good to ask for specific help and to have an awareness of being protected from others who aren't specifically able to be of the help you need. Never be fearful. Know that when you speak and call forth these helpers, it will be as you have asked. Your prayers protect you as if you were in a cocoon of light.

God, I feel I'm letting you down because I'm getting bogged down in things when I need to be listening more and organizing things and...

Anne, be gentle with yourself. I am here. Yet, you are trying to carry the burdens of the world on your shoulders. Hand me your burdens. Let me carry them for you. Relax all you can as you release all your burdens to me. When you have prayed and asked for my help and I take your burdens, do not take them back from me. Have faith that I will carry them, heal them and release them from you to free you. Then do what you are now free to do.

But, God, I feel old and tired and unproductive....

You feel old....

You have quite a sense of humor. I see what you mean. I've just been feeling sorry for myself. I can see that I need to get out of that state.

– ✡ –

I want to understand more about your love for all of us.

> Anne, I want us to tell everyone over and over and over that I love them. They have forgotten. Or if they remember, they think I love them only if they follow some arbitrary God-rules and thou-shalt-not-rules. When they don't follow what were never my rules at all, they think I withdraw my love.
>
> You know the love your daughter Debbie has for her daughter Krystalyn, and the love you have for both of them. You know the love you have for your other children and grandchildren, the love you have for Herb, for your mother, your sister and brother, your friends. This is a dewdrop in the ocean compared to the love I have for you, for each of you.
>
> I am not a person; but you can have a deeply personal relationship with me. A relationship greater than the grandest love affair you can imagine, stronger than

the dearest friendship, more than the unconditional love for your children, the deepest love you have ever felt and your highest aspiration. I can be all those things to you, and more, if you will let me.

One day you will all love yourselves and each other as I do.

I want that, God.

Then claim it.

Now, here is something else. Everyone hears me all the time. Some aren't aware of it, some think that small voice within them is just their imagination. But, that voice that answers the heart's desires and the mind's deepest seeking is *me*. I am with you always. I love talking with all my creation and you were created to hear and to talk with me.

MESSAGES FROM GOD

CHAPTER 2

...God speaks about...
women, men, children, homosexuality,
abortion, divorce...and clutter...

Anne, you are not a woman.

I'm not a *woman*?

No. You are a *soul* choosing to use the form called female - woman - for a time on this planet at this particular time period. Only in this experience are you a woman. When you return to me you are neither. You are a soul returning to your creator.

But, I like being a woman very much.

> Good. But don't like it too much. Earth is but a temporary home, as is this female incarnation.

Then, how can I help you write about a woman's messages from God when I'm not really a woman?

> Because while you're here, and when you return again and again, it's helpful and important to know how a woman feels, what her special roll is, how she can use her energies and talents to the fullest and what special help she can give to the world. And, it is sometimes different from the male thoughts and actions.
>
> See how masculine I sound to you because you associate what I said with men, the males. When I say something you associate with women, you hear me in a more feminine awareness. Then there are times when you hear me as neither - just as I AM.

Well God, as I see women doing what seem to be the jobs men have traditionally always had, the line between men and women blurs.

> Jobs, activities have nothing to do with one being male or female, or very little. There are some jobs taking much strength that cannot be done as easily by most women. But, as far as capability, most jobs can be done equally well by either. So, jobs are not what separate men and women.

Then what does?

> Let's talk about being in a woman's body. In some ways it is an incredible experience. Women have such

sensitivity, such awareness, and such love. You are able to create, and to carry another human in your form and to bring it to life. You have the power to create and to cause to live or die by small acts committed or acts you fail to commit. So, choosing to be a woman is choosing to be the more creative of the two sexes. Books like *Men Are From Mars, Women Are From Venus* are very helpful in understanding the differences between men and women; but, they lack the basic understanding that all souls *choose* the gender they need at the time to work out their individual lessons and experiences.

Though women can for the most part do anything men can do, why try to be like men, when the women's role is of such importance. Her role is far more effectively filled when she is not trying to compete, which is primarily a male characteristic.

Whatever state I am in, therein I have learned to be content. A powerful truth. You have chosen the female state, which is quite different from the state of a male. Therefore, great distress will be prevented when women are content in their state and don't try to become like men. An apple is a glorious creation - so is a peach. But, a peach trying to be an apple? What a waste of a good apple and of a good peach. See the humor in that; yet, see the truth.

Then, it is important to discover what is the woman's purpose. What she is here for that is different from men. How a woman can be the best woman she can be, and be herself, not being put down or stepped upon because she is not a man.

There is a specific purpose for women?

> Yes. A woman's purpose is to create - to create children (some women), to create stable happy homes where the male partner or children or other family members can be at peace and grow. A woman's primary purpose is to create harmony on the planet.
>
> Many women want to stay home, raise their children, prepare healthy meals, and teach their young all the best they know. But, society has in this time period caused such a work to be looked down upon. Some women will even deny that this is their deep desire, since their egos have been programmed to feel a career outside the home is the only worthwhile endeavor.
>
> Yet, I would say to you, what career is more worthwhile than their deep inner desires, which they work diligently to suppress? In fact, the more some protest, the stronger is this desire. But, they feel they must fight to be more than just a housewife. You ask how to heal this planet? Let the women who have the courage to do so begin to help rebuild it by establishing strong and loving homes and foundations for their children and families.
>
> It is not an easy job. It is far harder than running a corporation for which males get such acclaim for extra money for their stockholders. Yet, some of those stockholders get shot down in the street or mugged by children who had no foundation set for them by the women and men who could have created a child of light, instead of a child without purpose or character.

Chapter 2

Wait a minute, God. This is not going to be a popular stance.

> I have never tried to be popular - just truthful. And, I can be no less when you ask. Have any of the Christs I have sent been popular with their truths? You don't need to answer. They haven't, of course.
>
> If only the new generation could know that motherhood, wife-hood and home-hood (by that I mean, "carrying the mantel" and "chosen responsibility") are by far the most honorable of all the jobs on the earth. If they would become educated about these things from birth, through school and into adulthood when they choose, then you could see a planet beginning to be at peace and to recover from the ravages of wars, lack, hunger and rebellion.
>
> For those who must or feel they must work outside the home, it is a much more difficult job to raise the children in the most desirable way. It can be done; but it puts intense responsibility on the single parent or couple who do this. This is where an extended family should be treasured. Grandparents, aunts, uncles, cousins, friends can make the difference between whether a child grows up straight and strong or bent by negative outside influences.
>
> There has been a loss of honoring grandparents for their wisdom and caring. Small difficulties should be set aside for the good of the children. Let the grandparents nurture in their way and the parents in theirs. The combination, working in accord, can be one of the greatest gifts to a child. I am not suggesting there are not difficulties between generations at times. I am

saying that working these out can be so helpful to a growing child as to aid them in all they do the rest of their lives.

Hillary Clinton has the right idea - it takes a village to raise a child. And, when a parent can't raise the child, all family and extended family members and all in proximity of that child must take over. But more, even if the mother and father are raising the child in the very best way, all the extended family and friends should still consider it their responsibility, their great spiritual responsibility, to care for the child. They need to set good examples for it, and to help in any way they feel they can add to that child's growth and character.

Jimmy and Rosalyn Carter are those who are helping provide homes and much else for just such a transformation of consciousness. It is not my will that any of my children be homeless. No one deserves to be hungry. No one deserves to be without shelter. Sometimes individual's choices have created these situations; sometimes the choices of others have. It is the responsibility of each of you to help your brothers and sisters who do not or cannot help themselves fully.

You see when it concerns children and families, there is no party, no politics, no male-female division, no separation whatsoever. Your children are the gold ore just being mined and brought to the light to be polished and treasured. It is a sad mark on current society that most people treasure a piece of gold or a diamond or ruby more than a child who is a far greater treasure.

There is something else that women can do that would heal the current generation of children and those in generations to come. Thousands of women stay in marriages where they and their children are being seriously abused mentally, physically and spiritually. They do not take the responsibility for leaving or take measures not to tolerate the abuse. This often comes from what these very women saw their own mothers experience. They have not developed self-esteem or prepared themselves to support their children without the aggressor's help. They were never taught parenting skills, relationship skills or how to honor themselves.

By accepting and tolerating such abuse, women become equally responsible for this causing their children to often mimic the very behavior the aggressor exhibits. The children act out their pain during childhood and into adulthood. They continue the abuse with their partners, and sometimes it accelerates, for they have seen nothing else.

But God sometimes when women have the courage to leave they are murdered by the abuser. Some stay, knowing this can occur.

Yes, sometimes this does occur, and those of you who care must change the laws and change society's ideas about abuse to keep this from happening. Sometimes death is better than continuing in such a way. That's another subject, since most of you do anything to survive, to keep from dying. You do not yet see that death is a friend not an enemy.

Shelters and homes of all kinds need to be available to these women. They need to be required to attend classes to enable them to stay free from the consciousness that causes them to often return to the abuser. Their children need counseling with caring teachers so they don't grow up to be the abused or the abusers.

Now let me also show you the other side. The men who abuse are in great pain. They have either grown up watching such abuse, or failed to be taught wisely and develop character traits strong enough to learn to handle their anger and frustration in better ways. They too need help. Some of their programming is so deep they will not allow such help. Without this, they essentially fail to achieve any worthwhile growth during the incarnation and will return again to learn to deal with these issues.

It is a scar on your current society that anyone can abuse anyone whether male or female, child or adult and it be allowed. Those living in such situations are slaves and no one was created to be enslaved and abused. Laws must change and individual consciousness must change. Schools must teach young women and men about the sacredness of relationships and how to nurture them and how to be good parents and husbands and wives. These would be more helpful classes than many they are required to attend.

To think that most young people graduate from high school without such instruction is one of the saddest commentaries on your society. You must refuse to tolerate such poor education in things which matter. Young people are not taught how to interact in relationships, about honor, compassion, honesty, and those

> character traits that are far more important than algebra, for instance, which most seldom use.

It really is inexcusable.

> You, as women, can effect these changes far better than men. You can fight for and insist on those things your children need to be taught in school. You can see that they are taught at home, also, by you and by your partner or some family member or friend.
>
> Young people aren't even taught how to handle money wisely in preparation for when they live on their own. Because of this, when they move out and get in relationships, there is never enough money, because they never learned how to budget and spend correctly. Even when they make enough money, there is never enough, because of this lack of education. Students are taught how to add and subtract, but not how to balance check books, budget their money, and their time. This can be changed. Women and men working together can insist on changes in their children's education at school, and provide some of it at home. It will make such a major difference in the lives of all young people.

Sometimes, God, it's so discouraging, all the things that we and our society and world do incorrectly. There doesn't seem to be any hope for the massive changes that need to be made even for such basic things.

> Don't waste any precious time being discouraged. Take little steps to make changes in every way that you can, then take bigger and bigger steps. Consider your whole life sacred. You chose this life, and this time period, to

be of as much help as you can possibly be in the years you inhabit your earthly form. There is nothing else more important than becoming strong within yourself, and being of the greatest possible service in every way each moment of your life. You can experience that with hope and in joy.

I will try to remember all that. I will also try to remember that I am a soul, not just a woman.

God, when I thought this over, about not being a woman, I realized that it distressed and disturbed me because I am very attached to my gender. Even though I believe I've been here before, I can only comfortably allow memories of other female lifetimes. Occasionally a dream enters and I see myself as a male, but I rationalize it was only a dream.

You are not alone, Anne, in this limited and incorrect thinking. That you rationalize, "it was only a dream," is something we'll discuss later.

Good morning, Anne. Let's talk about clutter.

Clutter? God wants to talk about clutter?

Of course. Who do you think has inspired all the books on getting rid of clutter and simplifying your life?

You? Books like *Clutters Last Stand* and *Simplify Your Life*? You inspired these? They were great.

> Yes. I dislike clutter because I know how it gets a stranglehold on my creation and slows individual growth and planetary growth. Did you know that every war is fought because of clutter?

I thought wars were fought for spiritual principles and religious ideals?

> You would think so but that's only a cover for protecting clutter. Clutter is whatever you have that you don't need to live. Kingdoms fight to acquire someone else's clutter or to reclaim clutter that has been taken from them.

That's a different way to think of it.

> You are on your way to eliminating various kinds of clutter. Keep at it.
>
> Bit by bit, simplify. Organize, follow through. Throw out, give away. Order creates success; disorder creates confusion. Set your houses in order - first your physical body house, then the house you live in, then the facility where you work. 1-2-3. Order creates success. It allows my spirit to enter more easily.

Speaking of clutter, there are so many books to read. We have a library of books we have bought and can't get read. It's hard to get rid of any because they may contain valuable information. I can't keep up. Is there some way to get more reading done? Where do I start?

> I can help you declutter your library. I will bring books to you from time to time and direct them to you through others. Ask me and I will tell you whether I sent a

particular book to you. Sometimes I will see that you get a book in unusual ways. If you take time to ask me, I will also advise you if a book is of help at a certain time. If it isn't, put it aside and see if you are drawn to it later. You may never be. Ask me if there is someone who would be helped by the book and then give it to them.

Go in a bookstore or library and pause and ask me to direct you to a book that would be helpful at this time in your growth. There are times that not one book would be helpful and hopeful or would benefit your soul growth. Other times you may feel compelled to purchase or check out several. Place your hands over a book, and simply ask me. I will always tell you if you will listen. Easy, isn't it?

Some reference books and those that can be studied by yourself and others during a lifetime should be kept in your library. Most should be distributed to others so they can learn from the information in them. Ask me and I will be your "heavenly" librarian and help you get your clutter to someone who will benefit from it and treasure it.

Next morning I woke up hearing a voice, neither male nor female - "Clutter is clutter whether in a carport, house or yard; or in a mind." I didn't have to ask whose voice it was.

Chapter 2

– ✡ –

God, I am keeping my appointment with you. It's 5:00 a.m. and I have been awake since 4:30 a.m. I had to decide whether to sleep or to talk with you. I know how important our talks are. So here I am.

> Good morning, Anne. We met together last night as we have done every night since you were born. In the quiet as you sleep, we connect, for you have no barriers between us then. In truth I am with you 24 hours a day; but, in your busy-ness, you are usually not aware. When you sleep you are more aware of me, and we have our times of sharing and questioning and planning.
>
> When you are awake, you are always with people; and, you must meet yourself when you are alone with me. Part of you longs to be alone more, away from the hustle and bustle; but you also are so programmed to have people around that when alone there is a sense of deep loneliness early in the morning. You have some fear of being alone, dying alone, having no one, and your fears keep you even from me. These fears are shared by many.

– ✡ –

> You wanted to talk about the Ten Commandments which we will do more fully later, but let's address, "Thou shalt not commit adultery," first.

> In much of the very distant past almost everyone in a group or community or tribe mated with everyone else. There was not the understanding that the mating created a child; but it was felt that other forces did. Sex was simply enjoyed and children were born. As awareness and intelligence increased, family units formed, and relationships of the twos.

I had read something like that, but thought it was fictional.

> It wasn't. As time passed the evolvement of humankind created a different consciousness. Unions became stronger when there was monogamy although many still practiced polygamy. Polygamy is neither right nor wrong. Polygamy practiced now, with the current misunderstanding of women's roles, and the supposed superiority of the male, creates great emotional pain and confusion. It simply works more easily and far better for one man to be with one woman for a lifetime when possible. It does not make wrong those who have multiple partners, divorces, or remarriages. Nor does it make wrong those who make incorrect decisions to align with a partner, then discover they are not compatible and all affection is gone, then sever the relationship. There are variations on those themes; I do not judge these things. Neither should any of you.

> The way society is set up at present, when divorce occurs, and children are left behind, and there are remarriages, it is often very very difficult for the children. It would not have to be so, and it shows a great deal of lack of enlightenment, when adults unable to stay with a particular partner often turn children against the other partner. Then there becomes a tug of war for

the child's affection and loyalty. It doesn't have to be that way; and a select few do not allow that to happen. Generally the children of these severed unions adjust better and become better adults themselves when the parents act fairly toward each other.

Perhaps this will help. Every time one parent criticizes the other parent in front of the child, or the child overhears negative things said about a parent, the child processes the information that they themselves are like that parent. Those faults must be in them too, their minds rationalize consciously and unconsciously, because they were created by both parents and half of them is like each parent. So great care must be exercised if you are to create an emotionally healthy child and future adult.

What can be done?

Women must make the changes here. Especially women. For they have the most power to effect such a change. Women have fallen down on the job, and they often allow themselves to play into society's stereotypes of them. Then they fail to use their personal power to bring harmony and peace to their families and especially to their children.

Women are largely responsible for the way in which society has regressed so badly into crime and hatred. For, it is within the mother - the goddess - that there is the power to make havens of their homes, to inspire their children to greater character, and to become more fully productive and empowered themselves.

What about men? It seems they have done at least as much damage.

> Does it really? It is not a man's *major* role to make the home a haven. It is his role to provide and protect and to show by example the character traits that children should model. Not that some men do not create such a haven, and do this quite well, but they are the exceptions.

This is confusing. I thought you said men and women were equal and could do anything equally well almost - except for certain physical jobs.

> They *are* equal; their jobs are just different. Some men and women exchange roles happily; but, again, these are the exceptions. A woman can learn to do almost anything a man can do. But, her role when incarnating most often has a deeper and different meaning than that of a male.

Are there specific suggestions about what women can do or what men and women can do together to help change things?

> Individuals with the same ideal of service can band together in groups and the combined energy to accomplish and get things done is beyond measure.
>
> Look at the services a group of you provided for the homeless when you worked together as one.
>
> World hunger? Begin with one child at a time. Adopt and support a child through one of dozens of programs. Ask for reports on how the money the organization receives is distributed, and then make a deci-

sion which one to support. One child is fed this way. One child does not go to bed hungry. One person *can* do something. Adopt a second, a third, and a fourth child. Four children will not go to bed hungry.

While you're at it, encourage others to apply for and literally adopt one of thousands of children in foster care, orphanages, overseas or wherever children die unattended through lack of care. One child has a chance then. One child can be saved.

I'm not sure that I could adopt another child.

I didn't mean that *you* do this particular thing. You adopted two children years ago, and it made a difference in their lives far beyond what you understand. But, you don't speak out enough about adoption. Since you gave birth to two children, then adopted two, you could help couples and individuals better understand that they will love their adopted children exactly the same as their biological children. Children just need *someone* to *love* them. Blood relationships are of little importance. Besides, in truth all of you are adopted, since I am your true Father and Mother.

When you see children on the streets, needing homes, being abused and neglected, and your heart calls you to help them, know that they may have been your very own children once. You would not let your own child suffer so. Yet, you may be doing just that, for you see, *all* children are yours.

Help and support crisis centers and homes where abused women and children can escape to safety. Help women develop greater self-esteem so they will neither tolerate such abuse nor be examples for their children to perpetuate or be victims of such abuse.

Find causes that are worthy and that you believe in and adopt that cause as part of your spiritual growth.

I see what you mean God.

Good. You want to make a difference, change the world? One child, one person, one deed at a time will do it. Use your intuition as you seek out which thing or things you can do best. For you, personally, writing is part of what will make a difference, but it is not all you are called to or capable of doing.

What about abortion, God?

Abortion should not be used as a form of birth control. Abortion is a simple issue that has been made complex by people presuming to speak about it in my name.

This may bring peace to some – the soul does not enter the body, except on rare occasions, until the baby takes its first breath. Later I will explain to you how the soul chooses the parents. The soul is without beginning or end, so there are not young souls and old souls. The waiting soul is ever aware of the changing choices of the parents or mother. If it cannot enter at one time because the mother's body is unable to carry the developing fetus to full term, it will enter at another. It may return and enter into the next pregnancy or select another set of parents. If an abortion is chosen to terminate the pregnancy, for whatever reason, the same thing occurs.

That some people feel they remember being in the womb can either be imagination, which it often is, or there is the remembrance of being around the mother and father during the pregnancy. Sometimes the soul will take its consciousness into the uterus to check on the development of its vehicle. It never stays there for long periods of time.

It is good, once the parent or parents choose an abortion, for them to talk to the soul that would have entered. They can perhaps invite it to return at the proper time during a future pregnancy. The soul will then choose if that is a satisfactory decision and either wait or select other parents. The fetus is simply the shell or container that would have housed the soul while on earth.

This is not cold and clinical whatsoever. There is a constant spiritual process going on in the selection of the parents, and the parents allowing a soul to enter or not enter. I am a part of each step of that.

Is abortion spiritually or morally wrong or right? It is neither. It is the free will choice of the parents or the mother to decide whether or not a child is wanted at a particular time.

Those who would tell you that using birth control is wrong are speaking from their own or other's thinking, not my words. Those who say that abortion is murder are speaking from what they have been taught, not what I have taught.

Having a baby, allowing a child to enter and raising a child of God are holy responsibilities and a sacred trust. To allow a soul to enter a form and be born, then neglected, abused and destroyed is the real error. I do not say "sin" because the meaning of that word has been so altered. Sin always meant error and falling short of the mark. As in archery when an arrow misses the mark, one picks up the arrow and aims again until it hits the mark it was intended for. So, too, is that how I created you, never to quit or give up until you reach the mark you have aimed for.

Many times women have a longing to get pregnant and have a baby when what their soul is longing for is for them to be creative in other ways. Giving birth to a baby is a highly creative act. However, for many women this is not what she truly needs. If she is out of touch with her soul awareness, she may mistake her need to become more creative with wanting to get pregnant and having a child.

Almost every mother should be involved in some creative activity no matter how busy her life is. She should make time for those things that satisfy her soul's creative urges, or, as I said, she may desire to create a baby when it is not an ideal choice for her or her family. This activity can be painting, artistic activities of all kinds, gardening for some, writing, singing, or dozens of other creative endeavors. The next time you or other women you know start thinking how nice it would be to have a baby again, think on these things and begin some other creative activity to satisfy that longing.

You have but to look at the world and the overpopulation of countries who do not use wisdom in allowing the entering of children. They have often been taught that planning for a family is against my will and that I will provide no matter how many children they have. I cannot step in and intervene in their free will. I can only watch, as do you, the unnecessary outcome. Many of these children do not survive the first year, much less reach adulthood. Many starve or die of thirst. Is this a wiser way? It is not my will; it is not my way.

Some will be comforted by this. Some will call it blasphemy.

What do you call it?

I call it truth. Since we are discussing controversial topics, can you shed some light on homosexuality?

Homosexuality is not a controversial topic for me. Is it for you?

No, but it is for many. So I'd like to hear from you what you think about it.

I don't think about it more or less than I do about heterosexuality. What do you think I think about it?

I don't think you care whether a person is with the opposite sex or the same sex, if they are loving and caring with each other.

> I care that whatever choices you make, to be with the same or opposite sex, that you are loving and that you are growing spiritually. Since you are a soul and neither male nor female except for this incarnation, your choices or inclinations are your own decisions.
>
> Some of those sexual inclinations are from past sojourns on earth; others are from your childhood programming, or genetics. Genetics are strongly past life in origin but that's another subject.
>
> Can you imagine that I would punish, judge or withdraw my love from any soul because of their sexual orientation? Yet many believe I do. One day they will meet me face to face and see the error in their thinking. Almost all who judge those who are with one of their own sex, have had either religious or fear-induced programming from childhood.
>
> It is not my will that there be gay and straight communities divided thus. We are all one and this separates. It is understandable that those who have been oppressed band together, but the cause would be better spent in service to others without such divisions.
>
> Perhaps with all of you becoming aware of your oneness, there will be no more black and white, gay and straight, no we and they.
>
> If you but knew how many blacks have been brothers and sisters and loved ones to those fearful whites that

oppressed them. If you but knew how many of those who are homosexual have been mothers, fathers and loved ones to those who torment them. Reincarnation is the great leveler and we will talk about that soon. When those opposing each other leave their physical bodies and meet in the dimension you call death or the other side, they recognize each other and there are many tears and much pain.

Let me talk about AIDS since we are on these topics. I did not send this disease to punish those who have partners of the same sex. I do not send disease to anyone ever. This disease is part erroneous thought form, part hygienic imbalance against certain earthly physical laws, and partly the choice of individuals for learning or service. It usually occurs because of a combination of these three.

No one contracts the disease without allowing it. The individual may not be conscious they have done this, but on a subconscious or higher level, they have chosen to experience various degrees of the disease. Some do this to learn, some to help others.

This is not an unfair world. It is a *just* world when you understand the laws of the earth, body, mind and spirit, and the laws of reincarnation and rebirth.

That is quite a lot to process and understand, God. It feels correct, but it makes my mind race and play a hundred scenarios, and creates hundreds of questions.

I know. We have all the time in the world to talk about those questions.

– ✡ –

God?

> Yes, Anne?

Did I hear you say that instead of just preaching to or telling others, we all must lead by example, and live what we teach?

> Yes, in part. You must share with words, which you personally are gifted in doing. But you must lead by example. No words make up for failing to do what you preach to others. Therefore, the things I am sharing with you must be lived, not just listened to. When you share my words with others you must make my words living words, words that you by example personally live, if they are to mean anything. Then those in turn share my living words with others by the way in which they themselves live them. On and on it goes, seeding the world, planting hope, changing consciousness and creating the 100th monkey effect.

Do you want to explain the 100th monkey effect?

> Anyone who is ready to be part of this change can read Ken Keyes book, *The Hundredth Monkey*.
>
> Sleep well, we'll talk while you're asleep.

Goodnight, God.

- ✡ -

Good morning, Anne. I am pleased that we are talking more and that our conversations now have a higher priority in your life, instead of last place.

I certainly have missed out on lots of talks with you and have created a lot of stumbling blocks in my life by not seeking your guidance.

> Yes, and it is all so unnecessary when you realize you can learn lessons in easier ways. I did not create you to stumble and grow through pain. You *can* grow through pain, but I created an easier way - to grow through ease and joy. It's also a lot faster growth and progress. I did not create you to test you. Only a very unloving and unaware parent would test their children or friends. A good parent or friend tries to help their loved one learn from the difficulties, but does not test them nor delight in their pain.

Are you disappointed in what I've gotten done?

> Not disappointed my child. For you can take as long as you like. Rather, I see you are disappointed with yourself for all you have left undone. You cannot do it all, though you would like to; but you can do much. It would be better to stop wasting any time worrying about how old you are and the years you have wasted.

Think instead that you have many years yet to use your gifts to help others and enjoy life to the fullest.

Every year of your life you should consider yourself in the prime of life; and, every year the best year of your life so far. It's true, you really should ask yourself how old you would be if you didn't know how old you were...and if you didn't look into a mirror so judgmentally. Then act and be that age, as you perceive it. This is not denial. This is the way to live life without buying into the erroneous thought forms of aging that create such discouragement and fear.

When you are fearful, it is hard for me to get through the barrier that fear puts between us. For fear is like a wall; it comes between you and everything else, making clarity and decision-making difficult. Fear makes our communications difficult. Fear shortens earthly life. Fear immobilizes. Fear is not what I created my children to draw to them.

Are there lots of people you're talking to and teaching these things?

Everyone. All the time. Everywhere. Always. Do they all listen to me? No.

Some don't believe in me. Some believe but don't think I speak. Some believe I speak but don't believe they can hear me. Some hear me but don't believe it's me. Some believe it's me but doubt they are worthy to hear me. Some hear and believe but are afraid to tell others. Some hear, believe and tell others. Some believe but tell others things I haven't said. Some don't believe and tell others things I haven't said. Some hear, believe, tell others my messages and write what I share with them. I wish there were more of the latter.

You do have a great sense of humor, God.

– ✡ –

What would my life be like, God, if I listened to you every day of my life and asked your guidance in all decisions I made?

Bliss. Try doing it and you will understand what bliss is.

Is there a secret to using my time better and doing my life's work?

Create a strong foundation of faith so that the little things don't get you down. Read and watch only things which inspire and lift your spirit to me. Ask my help in all things. Even the small things. For instance, ask, "Is going canoeing good for today? Is this or that the best use of my time? God, what would you have me do? Is this food ideal for me at this moment? What is?" See? A God-directed, God-lived life. Then all the other will come. All the answers to all else will come as a natural follow-through of such a way.

I understand.

Then begin today. Ask me and I'll answer you every time. If I know the number of hairs on your head, and I do, don't you know how much I love and care for you? And, how much I love and care for each of my creation.

— ✡ —

God, any words of wisdom today?

> Persevere, Anne, my dear child. You get an A for effort but not quite so high for application.
>
> Remember that I use imperfect channels like you. It is the message that is important, for my messengers are imperfect.
>
> I know you are concerned because you have great plans and take little action. You get busy and caught up in other things. You can do that; but it is not the best way. Listen to what I would say to you. I will use you and work with you as I have with others. My hand is upon you. Begin today anew. Each moment is truly a new beginning. Trust my ways and expect the things you have chosen. Act as if you already have them. Know you cannot fail. You can only delay your good.
>
> Let me lead you. Overcome your fears. Get up early each morning and talk with me. Every day. Reconstruct your life, as you have desired to do. I will help you each step of the way. I can talk to you at any time, anywhere; but, when you keep our scheduled appointments, you listen more clearly and fully and trust more surely.

God, why don't I do what I know to do?

> You are not focused my child. Make it easy for yourself to succeed. Relax your self-imposed rules.
>
> Bring forth the truth - that I love talking with my own, that I would never create you and leave you without a way to know me and to talk with me and to hear me. I created you - all of you. How do you feel about *your* children? Well, so do I. I care. Just as you care or could care. I see you as souls, with all your strengths; for weaknesses are only strengths unrecognized. I want you to succeed not fail. I want you to be filled with power so we can create together. For you are both the created and the creator.

How do I create?

> With every thought and action you are creating good or ill for yourselves and others. If you create that which lifts up and try to avoid that which tears down, the world becomes an Eden, not a hell. An ill thought or action does no one any good; but a good thought or action creates a world in love, at peace. No easy earthly lesson, yet learned, transforming.

God, why can't I see you?

> Anne, you *can* see me. Look in the mirror. Look at everyone and everything around you. You see me. I am in you and in everyone and in all things. You are created in my image – look at all of creation and you will see me. Touch the hand of someone and you have touched me.

— ✡ —

I hate coming back in another body next lifetime and having to do it all over again, yet, I can see I'll have to. It is scary to think about being trapped in a child's body for several years.

> Yes, it can be dangerous and frightening. It is also not exactly as you think. We'll talk about that sometime.

Then how can I lose my fear and do what I have came in to do now, and not worry about something in the future?

> Live life fully now. Do what you know to do *now*.

— ✡ —

God, I have a fear that if I do well this lifetime, I'll die and leave sooner; but, if I don't do things well I will get to hang around longer to get it all done.

> A groundless fear, which many have. Success is a beginning, not an end. It is to be enjoyed. You will live far more fully by allowing yourself to accomplish all you are capable of doing. Use your gifts to help me help others. Worry not how long you will live; but concern yourself with how well you use every moment of your life.

— ✡ —

Chapter 2 57

God, how can I be sure it's you and that I'm not being misled?

> Anne, you know it's me. You know you are not being misled by the way our conversations make you feel. Your soul knows. I will come to you tonight and rest upon your heart and soul; and, you will awaken knowing without any doubts.

– ✡ –

Thank you, God. I woke up feeling absolute peace. You're right – *I know.*

That peace and knowing continue to this day.

– ✡ –

When is the best time to listen to you, God?

> Any time you feel the need to talk with me; but also, when you are totally quiet and alone. The Millennium must be ushered in by messengers such as those of you who answer the call. For many are called and few answer. Each of you is my messenger already, but not to the extent you could be if you really let me direct you.
>
> Write this book with me because your soul calls you

to write it. Write our book to remind my people of my love and promises. This book is complete in spirit already. Now complete it in your dimension. It will encourage others to talk with me. Our talks together will help them heal and then can help in the healing of this planet.

God, is there anything special you want to tell me today?

> Just that I love you, that's all.

I love you too, God.

> I know you do, Anne.

God, as if you didn't know, Herb just gave me a neck, head and back massage, I feel so much better.

> Touch, human touch, with a loving spirit, is a great gift from one to another. I will talk to you more about the need for all to have physical contact and touch, and how this can be done in a variety of ways.
>
> Husbands and wives should touch frequently and lovingly. Children should be touched and loved constantly. People are starved for human touch. Because

some have touched others in ways that cause emotional and physical pain, many people are uncomfortable with touching others or being touched. The touch from someone who cares for you is healing and uplifting.

Massage can fill the void many have for that healing touch, as well as being therapeutic in many other ways. Learn from your neighbors in Japan and other countries who practice Shiatsu and massages on their whole family. Massage and touch your newborns and children of all ages. Keep hugging your children no matter what ages. It will keep you young and keep them closer and more bonded to you as adults. Children begin to withdraw from kissing and hugging at certain ages, partly because of their peers, but embrace them through these stages.

Your elderly long for attention and touch. Hug them, embrace them whenever possible. Get massages for them to ease the hunger for touch they feel.

Lay your hands on someone's arm in a caring touch, pat someone on the back. Do it in my name and stop being fearful you will be accused of sexual harassment. Err on the side of tenderness and touching.

God, I am concerned about women's issues, but also about all of humankind's issues. I have some ambivalence about how active a role to take in the women's movement.

Women's issues of all kinds are important, for they are humankind's issues, just geared to help women become empowered. Women must become fully empowered if the world is to be in harmony this Millennium.

Those in women's bodies, those of you choosing to express and learn as women, have such a struggle with how you look that it bogs you down in all you do. This is society's programming, not mine. Women should not be defined by their looks, age or occupation. Nor should they limit themselves because of their gender. Nor should they be overbearing because of their gender.

For those of you having difficulty now with the opposite sex may well find yourselves switching roles in the next incarnation. Remember you are not women. You are souls experiencing this incarnation as female for lessons you need to learn, and strengths you need to acquire. You are here to do it with a sense of joy and purpose.

In ancient times those experiencing life called to the Mother-God for all their help, and honored her, making the men feel inferior. For wasn't *Mother*-God *female* and they were men or males? Then, since your conscious memory, those incarnate called to the Father-God. Generations of women have felt inferior. For wasn't *Father*-God *male*? Men, because of their work of writing and recording, and lack of awareness, wrote of women as less-than or inferior to men, thereby perpetuating the great untruth.

Now comes the dawning of Mother-Father God, in this Millennium. When it is not Mother or Father but I AM, for I AM means you recognize your role as Creator and created, then the Millennium can come in on winged feet and all will know me as friend. No one will go to another for guidance for all will hear and know me and I AM will be the call and the answer.

Then will you call me friend and there will be no "them" and "us" or men and women separate because of their gender and divided consciousness. All will know each to be one and all a part of each other and war will be no more. Our planet, beloved Earth, will be healed. Its scars will fade and new life will abound. If it were not so I would not tell you that it is.

I would that each would come to me daily as friends. Let us talk together. It is true that the greatest soul realization is that I speak today to men and women as in times of old, as I always have, as I always will.

You will hear me repeat these things, and many others, over and over again until you truly hear them.

Just as much makes no sense without fuller understanding, the fact that you have been here before and will return again makes no sense for those who feel I'm in a heaven *up* somewhere. I am in a heaven *here* with each of you. Yet, most of your brothers and sisters make of existence a hell, or what they feel hell is like. I would that you show them that heaven is within each of them if they will claim their relationship to me as it truly is.

MESSAGES FROM GOD

CHAPTER 3

...discussions with God about death, suicide, angels, the afterlife, prayer, and souls of animals...

God, how is Stephen?

(My son Stephen took his own life when he was 15 years old.)

Ask him yourself Anne. He's here with me, and with you.

Stephen how are you?

I'm fine Mom. I love you.

I love you too honey.

Grandmother is here. (My mother had died recently.) She is fine. She rests and reads a lot. She knows she is dead but doesn't want to think so much about it right now. You know how she always avoided stressful topics. So when she wakes and we begin to talk, she excuses herself very often and goes back to sleep or rests. She has a lot to unlearn but even more to process. No suffering as such, but not quite ready to take the next steps.

Mom, you do hear me a lot. Sometimes, no matter how I try, I can't get your attention. Don't stop listening, because I have so much to tell you and so much to help you with. I need your help to reach kids and stop them from killing themselves.

Stephen, I miss you.

I know Mom. But I can see you, I can hear you and I can read your thoughts. And you can hear me and feel me around you.

Yes. Sometimes I can, but I would rather you were here with me.

I would rather be there too Mom, but because of the decision I made to kill myself, that's not possible. We both must learn to communicate in this new way. I want to tell you about suicide more fully. Teenage suicide will be shown be the number one cause of death of young people one day. It actually is now, some statistics to the contrary. So many accidents with one teenager in the car are actually suicides. They even leave notes about their intent; but, to spare the family pain and embarrassment, they are ruled "accidents." Thousands of suicides of young people in their homes and elsewhere are also ruled accidents, even if there are notes and much evidence to the contrary, because there is still such shame and stigma attached to suicide.

Not only are thousands of deaths unreported suicides, but also *most* deaths are a form of suicide. When you smoke, drink, take drugs, or eat, breathe or touch things that you know are harmful to you, it shortens your life. These choices may create disease and illness, which can *quickly* shorten your life. When you take foolish chances that endanger your life, drive when drunk or impaired, play foolish games in cars, boats or planes and dozens of other things, it can easily result in death. Sometimes taking these actions is a conscious death wish, sometimes more subconscious. Nevertheless, it is a form of suicide. By choices, incorrect choices, and self-created illnesses you shorten your earthly life span. People are quick to judge overt suicides from guns, hanging or razors. They excuse themselves and others who die through the slower forms of suicide brought on by their own behavior and choices.

Hardly any of us who take our lives really want to die. We just want to stop the pain. At the time suicide seems easier than enduring the pain we don't know how to handle. Kids who kill themselves under the influence of drugs or alcohol don't always have a death wish as many think. They simply don't realize the ways these substances will affect them and cause them not to think clearly. They lose control over their actions.

I heard a woman whose son had recently killed himself tell you, "Maybe our children kill themselves because they don't know how much we love them." I knew you loved me; but it was only after I had taken my life and visited with you that I realized how *much* you loved me, and how much the rest of the family loved me. At the time I ended my life, I wasn't thinking about anything but the pain I felt. I didn't realize it would pass.

> For those like myself who didn't do drugs or alcohol, we just let the stress and depression of adolescence weigh us down until the pain was overwhelming. We all regret what we've done immediately, when we find ourselves in another dimension, which you call death or the spirit plane. Then we try to discover ways to let you know we're OK. Often no one listens. There's no hell or punishment here except what we feel inside when we realize what we've done.

Stephen, I keep remembering the dream from the other night where you were a little boy and came toward me to hug me. You were wearing a black bathing suit. It made me miss you so. I have had two really rough days, crying and sad because it's March 18 and the anniversary of your death.

> Mom I'm so sorry you're sad. I made such a horrible mistake, taking my life, yet I also see it can have a greater purpose. I have been allowed to contact you and others from this dimension. You can use my foolish action and your pain to bring help and understanding to so many people. Not just the people who write and call, but the thousands who read our book and don't write or contact you. Write and call those who contact you, with caring and compassion. They need to talk with someone so desperately.
>
> Mom, I was with you in the dream you had of me when I was younger. It was partly to show you that I was and still am loving and caring. The dream also showed you the stress that came from the years with the man, my stepfather, who abused us all. You pretty much interpreted the dream correctly.

Why black bathing suit pants?

> They symbolized unrecognized truth about our relationships from past lives.

Did I dream of you last night, also?

> Yes and no. You remembered part of a larger dream, about many other things; but we did meet and talk.

Stephen I heard a very well known and seemingly very accurate psychic say that people who committed suicide had to turn right back around and come in again to get it right. Several people whose loved ones took their own lives were very discouraged about this statement and want to know if it's true.

> Mom, it's usually not that way. Occasionally someone is allowed to return very quickly because of extenuating circumstances; but as a rule souls need quite a bit of time in this dimension to prepare for a return. Without counseling, an in-depth review of their records and an understanding of what led them to commit this act, their odds of it happening again when they return are very high. Even then a pattern has been set that will need to be met again when they return; and it may be even harder to choose another course than suicide again.

Son, I am so sorry for all the things I did and didn't do that caused you to hurt so much you wanted to die.

> Mom, it was my choice and my choice alone to kill myself. I forgive you and Dad and everyone else for the parts you played throughout my life. I had some character flaws that had nothing to do with you. I can help from here now. I am

allowed to talk with and visit all the people who have read our book and write you; and I have with a great many of them. The reason I am allowed is to try and comfort them because of their pain and sadness and to bring them some new understanding. Some I can help, some I can't.

I often meet with teenagers, like I used to be, who are thinking of killing themselves. There are times that I can impress on them not to take their lives; but, many times they do complete the suicide. When this occurs, I am with them as they release from their bodies and enter this dimension. This is not such an easy job, as you might imagine. Not only do I replay my own death, but I feel their pain as they commit the act and realize what they have done. I know what the pain of their families will be, just as it was for all of you; and that is very difficult.

I know you don't feel you are consistent in listening to me. I have it so much better than what most souls in this dimension experience when they try to talk with their families and no one listens. It is heartbreaking for them to be unable to talk with their loved ones. Many of their families don't even believe talking with the dead is possible, or worse, they are afraid it's somehow evil. So I'm one of the lucky ones.

One more question Stephen. God brought you to talk with me just now. Do you see and talk with God?

I see God all the time - when I look at myself and when I look at everyone else. We are all part of God and we are all God, yet there is also a part of God separate from us. I know what Moses must have felt. There is such power it engulfs you like a cloud surrounding you and you become one with it. Then it's like you're in a spinning cloud only not dizzy and you know that you and God are one.

It is hard to describe but that's my best way of using words to tell you. It is awesome. It makes you know you can do or be anything you want and it will all be right. When I first arrived here, I wasn't aware that I could talk with God anytime I wanted and he would answer me. I have learned a lot and grown a lot in these years.

Even though you talk with God, as we do, the experience is more intense and somewhat different in this dimension.

Do you see angels and talk with them?

Let me tell you about angels. They are wonderful! Some of them actually look like they have wings of shimmering beautiful colors, but that is really more like human auras. They teach us in different classes. Some are much like people you know, but they have incredible powers. They can look into your eyes and impress information and love and feelings and visions. They never have negative or mean thoughts, you can tell. They radiate only good and also a kind of peace, joy, love mixture that just makes you feel like a million dollars. It's hard to describe. It isn't as intense as communication with God. It is fantastic though.

I also meet lots of our relatives and friends who have died. I get to visit with people who are still alive and wandering around while their bodies are asleep. Some who died, I knew when they had bodies; some I recognize from photos you had when I was a child. We have lots of discussions and share information about what's going on and what we're up to.

> Mom - talking with me doesn't take away from talking with God - it's two different things mostly. All of us can talk with God. I can talk with you about teenage suicide and grief and all that. God talks to you about God-stuff, I guess.
>
> OK, Mom. I've got to go. I'll talk with you later.

Bye, honey. God thank you for letting me talk with him.

> Anne, my child, you must continue to teach others so that they too can commune with their loved ones who die.

I will.

> You can get to the point of awareness that when anyone dies there is the absolute knowing that you can have an even deeper experience with this one in the spirit plane. Yes, you will miss the physical body and touch, and the conversations you shared. But, you and the one you care for will be able to meet in other dimensions. There will be no feeling of loss. You will know that the soul is just in another room of the same house you are in. Maybe they won't often be back in the living room where you have been used to visiting them, but there are eight other rooms in the house where you can visit. You begin to see how grief can be transformed by awareness. Just as your computer is capable of so much more than most are currently aware.
>
> Stephen can still visit you in the living room, but usually you don't see him in the way he was in an earth

body and physically in the living room. He can be there nevertheless, in his spirit body. Or you go into the dining room and though you can't see him, you can sense his presence. You cannot embrace him and you cry because he's not in his physical body in the living room like you would prefer and were used to. You can learn to delight in your visit in the dining room, and begin to communicate and experience his presence in a different way there. Sometimes the dining room is too busy or other people are there so you make an appointment to meet in the kitchen, and you visit him there.

Different rooms are used for different things. As you allow yourself to sense and experience his presence in new ways, you find that you can visit in many rooms. Each room is connected to the house and you can freely go from room to room. It is like when your children were little. If they didn't answer, and you couldn't find them in one room, you searched the house until you found where they were. It is just easier to cook in the kitchen than the bathroom, more comfortable to lie down to sleep on the couch than in the basement, and easier to sit and visit around the dining room table than in the bathroom. You may always wish that you could have those hugs and conversations in the living room and hear that loved one speak out loud. However, as your awareness expands, you learn to hear in new ways, visit in different rooms and continue your relationship in deeper ways.

That's a good way to describe it.

Chapter 3

Stephen abides with me. His story is far from finished. Be his voice, that his act of pain and desperation may serve to warn and help others. He is beloved here as there. He has been a beacon of light to so many already. You hear him; but he is far more involved in your life than you are yet aware. Let him speak with you daily so that he and his helpers may help others through you. My hand is always on him.

Now, let me talk a little more about suicide. Suicide is very misunderstood. Ask yourself the question when you wonder about the soul of your loved one who took their own life, "What would a loving God who created my loved one do, when that loved one was in such pain that they killed themselves." Look into your heart and soul for the answer. You will find it. The answer will be, "A loving God would love them."

Many call suicide "self murder" but that is incorrect. You are gifted with a body to have an earth experience. What you do with it is entirely up to you. Your plan, before entering, was to treasure the experience and do good works. Your free will enables you to choose how you care for the body, mind and spirit. Your body is a gift; but like any gift, once it is given, you, the recipient, are free to do with it as it you will. If, however, you take the life of another it may rightly be called "murder" because that body was not yours to do with as you will.

Often, when returning in another body after taking your own life, much karma needs to be met because of all the lives that choice impacted upon. Almost no one, who takes their life in a moment of anger or pain, and returns to me, is ever glad they did what they did. The only exceptions to this are those who takes their own lives rather than betray comrades, friends or country, such as in military service. Or, those who do so to keep from being tortured, raped or murdered. Most of the terminally ill or elderly who decide to take control of their deaths when their quality of life is intolerable or they know their work is finished, do not regret their decisions.

God, Stephen told me about his grandmother, my mother. Can you tell me how she's doing now?

> Your mother is with me. She talks with me as she had often prayed to do when in her physical body. She is adapting to her new location, where many aid her and help her understand and adjust more fully. After she died, you did hear her speak to you. Sometimes you have an awareness of those who are dead, and that was one such time, when you heard her voice.

I had said to my mother a few months before she died of cancer from smoking, "What if I'm right mother, and when you die you're fully aware on the other side and meet all your loved ones who have gone before you?" She said, "I don't believe that way, but I hope you are right." Two days after her death, I was standing by the window where she had died in bed, praying for her. I distinctly heard her say two times, "You were right. You were right."

- ✡ -

> Stephen has always been with me, from the moment he made the decision to take his life because of his inner pain. He made a decision based on fear, from his low self-esteem, but not a decision of evil or such. He has talked with you often and most of what you have recorded is correct. There is much more. Stephen continues to aid many from his dimension and is constantly interacting with yours. He not only talks to you but to many others. He can take you on a walk through his dimension, and you could write about it. *A Walk Through Heaven,* you could call it. Just focus on what others need and want to learn and he will help you.

What do people need and want to learn?

> A faith to sustain them, hope that they and their loved ones continue after death and to know of my love for them. So many children and adults in the dimension you call death would like to bring messages to their loved ones in the earth plane. These loved ones just need reminding that it is possible to talk to those who have "died." I created a universe where there are no walls between dimensions, except of their own making. I would not create a world where death separates or there were no ways to keep in touch with

loved ones as they change form. They need to be reminded of that.

Live so fully, that when you die the work you came to do is finished. Then you can begin another step of this fabulous soul journey. We are never apart. You are trying to "find" me, and I have never left you. The masters such as Jesus never leave either; they work even more fully when released from the physical form.

What about animals? Do animals have souls or what happens to an animal when it dies?

They are always watched over by those in another dimension – even when alive: The Caretakers in that dimension watch over them much like angels watch over you. Many of these Caretakers are souls who no longer have or choose to have earthly bodies. They love animals and ask to be assigned to this particular mission.

I see.

All their earthly life, animals are watched over - monitored - by those in that dimension to which they will return. Sometimes it is these very Caretakers who alert the animal to awaken a family in case of a fire, not just the dog's instincts. Animals, like all living things, have souls that exist in that dimension but not as the human soul. They return to that dimension in a different consciousness when the physical experience ends, where they gather with others like themselves. They can experience other species in evolution, but mostly they return in their own species.

To a great extent those who guard the animal kingdom, especially those who oversee the animals that will be associated with the human kingdom, choose the person or persons to raise this pet. This is not based on the soul needs of the animal but the needs of the human. Not so with humans. It is a two-way adoption there. The incoming soul and the family it will enter both choose or allow or even at times *ask* for the association for *both* to learn from.

By the way, we had such fun creating this planet, the animals, bugs, growing things, humans, minerals.

What do you mean, *we*?

I God am *we*, not he or she but *we*. Many of us worked to make the earth the Eden it was and can be again. I God am *you*, I God am each of you, and *we* created this world and many others.

What do you mean many other worlds?

There are other worlds where there is no war, no want, no anger, no fighting, and the inhabitants enjoy life to the fullest.

I'd like to go to such a place.

You have been to these places. All of you incarnate

have. It is for this reason many feel such divine discontent so many times in a body, on this planet. You have a vague remembrance. You also travel to those places both during your sleep and at other times when you rest and meditate deeply.

There are also places of constant war, dark places where there is very little light and the souls there live in what you would call a hell. It is not where I send someone, but where souls place themselves because of their choices, and go as drawn to a magnet. They have the free will to choose another place, but the pull is so strong they flow with the pull and get bound into those energies. Always there are beings of light who try to help them release and make further growth in an easier environ.

God, tell me some more about death.

When people fear death, it immobilizes them. It not only makes them fearful to take chances, fearing to die, but fearful to do much of anything. There is such a feeling that death is the end, and what's the use of learning, because it is all wasted when you die. Or, that they are too old and why bother. What I want to tell you is that nothing - *nothing* is lost. Everything learned is saved and processed and stored, first in your mind as if it were a giant computer with a huge memory - a limitless memory in fact, then filtered to each cell of your body. When you release from the physical form, it is as if the hard disc goes with you, with all the stored memories and learning.

Now, the fact that you don't remember some past lives and other information that you *know*, is the evidence of such a small percentage of the mind being used, while in a physical body. When you do use more of your "mind" and that is not the correct term really - more of your memory storage bank or awareness - then you think miracles are occurring. It is just that you have accessed documents that you couldn't find before, sometimes containing a great wealth of knowledge and information and power.

Is it really possible to change the mess the world is in, and if so, what can I, as a woman, do to help?

It's really possible Anne; and, there is a lot you can do to help as a woman, as a person, as a parent and grandparent. You and thousands of others, both men and women can do this. First, you must personally have the courage to break free of any self-imposed limitations. Be daring. After all, who cares what anyone thinks about you? That is so very unimportant. Care only of our relationship; and, do what your soul calls you to do. Listen to and be led by your soul; and, don't be limited by the mind and body, which will hold you back. The soul will race forward, the mind and body will often hesitate.

> You are capable of anything you truly desire to do, anything you set as a goal for yourself. *Anything.*

Anything, God? Gymnastics come to mind. There isn't any way I could become a gymnast.

> Yes, you could. However, given an overall evaluation of your physical condition at this point, it would take a lot of work and commitment. It would take perseverance and some pain, but yes, you could become a gymnast. The question is: Do you really want to be a gymnast and are you willing to do what it would take to become one? The answer in you is "No," but you see the power available to you in just *knowing* it is possible. Now think of several things that you *do* want to do.

I want to write more books, continue to travel all over the world and lecture, be a good artist, paint and sketch, learn to dance well. Be a really loving and playful wife, mother, grandmother and friend.

> Well, you *can* do *all* these things if you truly want them. Set your goals. Do not falter. Affirm daily by your actions and progress toward these goals that you *will* accomplish them. See yourself accomplishing them. Act as if you have *already* accomplished all of them. Do you believe I can help you do this?

Yes, God.

> You must *know* that I can. People pray for help about thousands of things and are angry that I don't seem to answer, but it takes both of us to re-create. You *want-*

> *ing* to and *inviting* me to help gives me permission to work along side you in helping make these changes and accomplish what you desire. I have given you free will, and even I cannot go against your free will. I can't help, however, even if invited, if the individual does nothing and expects me to do it all.

I understand that.

– ✡ –

God, my friend just lost her father. She wants to know how he is.

> Anne, no one *loses* anyone. Her father shed his earthly form and changed dimensions. A more accurate thing to say when there is a death, is, "My father changed form, released from his physical shell and returned in his spiritual body to his awareness of oneness with his creator.
>
> About her father, the joy and peace and playfulness that eluded this one while in the recent physical form has been restored to him. It was lacking only because his childhood erased the playfulness; and, now, he plays as a child - with wild abandon and freedom.
>
> It is as if a terrible weight has been removed from his back; and, he can allow himself to stand tall, and enjoy life once more. It did not take long for him to become aware of where he was and to accept help, because deep within he had a loving heart.

Now he is attending school, and in his classes and learning, reviewing his recent life, and others. He will grow more rapidly from that understanding when he returns in another physical form at the correct time. He will return as a female, since he sees that he needs to learn greater sensitivity. He has asked not to return until his wife joins him. They will have time in this dimension to enjoy all the things that they were unable to enjoy together while in the earth plane.

He is not of the consciousness to be able to aid or help much from his dimension; but, he does visit his family, assisted by a helper, many times. He is preparing a place for his wife; and, they will both return together. She will incarnate in a male form to work out issues they hadn't resolved. Hopefully they will grow in ways they failed to do while together in this life.

The daughter who asks about him has the ability to work with those who have transitioned. She can help them release from ties holding them on the earth plane, ties of their own creating. She can also help those who are dying and fearful to release from their earthly form. As a nurse, she has gifts of healing and compassion as well as having a pure heart and truly good intentions. This will enable her to be of greater service in the future. In addition, she is a powerful prayer. She, like you, is quite capable of hearing me speak. Tell her that.

– ✡ –

Chapter 3

Is it true that prayer can sometimes cause things to be un-created, such as an accident? Can so much prayer be said that it causes time to go backward to the moment before the accident and it doesn't occur?

> Yes, my child that does upon rare occasions occur. When the energy of the pray-er is of such power and faith that it can interrupt and reverse time, it can happen.

How is that possible?

> Do you remember reading about going forward and backward simultaneously if enough power and speed are generated? Well, prayer and thoughts can be of such power as to take one back or forward in time. Something created can be un-created, and life continues on, because that event had not yet impacted on many others. It would be extremely difficult for most of you to create the kind of power to un-do, so to speak, something that had happened and the repercussions were already being felt by many. Jesus and some others could do this.

Did my prayers do that for my daughter who almost had an accident?

> No, but when you saw her you became aware of this possibility because you have sensed it could actually happen. You remembered from deep in your memory bank, from other times and from the times between lives when you were more consciously aware.

– ✡ –

God, you said you would explain a little more about angels, spirit plane guides and all that. Why are they needed when we have *you*?

> That has been a question for which many of you have long wanted an answer. These helpers are needed because so many will not believe in me. Many don't feel they are worthy to talk to me directly no matter how much I try to tell them differently. Angels and spirit plane guides can be my mediators, my assistants, to help others return to their awareness of our *oneness*. They have different assignments and different energies or vibrations and their work varies.
>
> Call upon them to help, and acknowledge their presence. Work with them and let them help you. Ask them questions and keep a journal with both your questions and the answers they share. Record the visions that come into your mind, and the impressions you receive. At times, ask how you can best help them to help you. Request to specifically meet with them when you sleep, are at rest or in meditation.

I'm still not sure how it works.

> Let me explain it to you in ways to make it clearer. Think of a large corporation. There is the CEO or chairman, or president of the board. I know there are sometimes all three, but for this example, let's say there is one top position, and I occupy that position. Under me there are vice-presidents and let's imagine that Jesus, Yogananda, Buddha and others who have

worked hard and measured up occupy those positions. Under them are the directors of different departments, who have special assignments. These are the archangels that you are familiar with – Gabriel, Michael, Uriel, Rafael and others. Each of these has hundreds of managers under them. These managers are the hosts of angels, the enlightened ones, all with different job descriptions. The managers have thousands of employees they are responsible for. These employees are you and the rest of the inhabitants of planet earth. Some of these employees have physical bodies, like you. Some have discarded the body and work from the spirit plane and other dimensions. I have grouped all of these employees under the same heading. This should show you that there should be no barriers between the living and the dead. There are many more positions and varieties of job being done; but this will suffice for what you are asking.

So I can talk to you anytime or to many of the others, too?

Yes, you can always talk to the CEO, chairman, or president. Always. I'm always available. You might say I manage my time well and always have time for appointments with all of my creation. But there's a lot of work to do. A lot of people need individual help. There is much work and many projects that need supervision. The archangels go out on larger-scale projects. While they, like myself, can be communicated with directly, their main assignment is overseeing projects like world hunger, peace and educational and spiritual endeavors. The angel hosts, with their varying job descriptions, help individuals and individual projects. You can talk with any of them.

> I assign to each of you three angels when you are born. One is a guardian angel, who will assist you during the entire earthly sojourn. One is an angel that has been with you for a very long time, through many other experiences and is the keeper of all your records and memories, so to speak. The other is a warrior angel whose energy is stronger than the guardian for protection and support in trials and turmoil. Now, they don't have feathered wings, but when you are able to see them, the aura or energy emanating continuously around them is wide and constantly moving and flowing.

I never believed angels had feathered wings. Now I understand why several angels that appeared to me *looked like* they had wings of some kind.

> Artists in other times portrayed them with wings, which isn't a bad idea actually, to distinguish them from mortals. However lovely the wings are sculpted and painted, they are not wings at all. They are simply energy fields. These three angels are always with you. So, know that in your loneliest moment, in your times of greatest despair, you are never alone. Not only am I with you, but these three never leave your side. And, others are drawn to you because of your needs.

> There are hosts of other angels that must be called upon if you want them to help. You may request them yourself, or ask me to send them to you. They will not intrude on your free will and they will come only when invited. As an example, there are angels of parenting, whose assignment is to help bring out the best in parents as they interact with their children. When you

feel you are unable to be the best mother or father you can be, and need help, call on them. You will know they are there by the peace you feel when you do this, and by the thoughts that come to you of ways to work more effectively with your children.

There are, among thousands of others for instance, angels of education.

Angels of education? That sounds strange.

Not really Anne. Children can be taught to call in these angels to help them with assignments. No, they won't do them for the child, but will help bring out of their memory information that will help them, and use thought to direct them to other help. Sometimes, Anne, you used to say, "God help me," when you were struggling with some homework or lessons, and that call allowed me to send these angels to you. Don't you remember how it would suddenly get easier and clearer?

As a matter of fact, God, I *do* remember; but I never realized what had happened. You mean that there were angels there helping me all the time?

Not all the time, but a lot of the time. There are angels of relationships, for instance. These can be called upon to help when you are having conflict in friendships, marriage and work situations. Some angels are assigned to churches, chapels, temples, mosques and synagogues. You can often make a contact with them and they will tell you what they do in that particular spiritual sanctuary. There are angels assigned to great mountains, to streams, to almost everything and everyone you can imagine.

I once saw an angel that filled the whole ceiling of my bedroom and a few minutes later I saw a band of smaller angels fly across the room. The large angel spoke to me but the smaller ones didn't.

> That angel was assigned to the work you and Herb are doing. As you know, it came to tell you what and how the work could be helped. The smaller angels simply were drawn by the power of the great angel and came to join in what was going on and add their energies to the experience.

That's amazing God. So, we are surrounded by these unseen angels on assignment from you, and sometimes called by us, all our lives?

> Something like that Anne. Then there are spirit plane guides. There is often confusion here; but I will explain it briefly. When you die, the energy contained in the envelope that is your body is freed, and expands out of the body; and, the body is discarded. That energy is moving faster than the molecules in the body, and cannot easily be seen, although, when it makes its release, some in the room can see it moving up and away from the body. Everyone thinks the body is dead and the person they knew is gone. This couldn't be further from the truth. The shell is discarded; the spirit is free and is taken or moves to a dimension where other souls reside. The full consciousness and awareness continues; so the soul energy doesn't feel "dead" at all but vibrantly free and light.

Some of those souls have made such progress while encased in a body, that they choose to stay in the dimension and vibration closer to those still living in bodies, to help them. Others go elsewhere. I will talk to you about that later. Those who stay close are sometimes assigned as helpers or, if you will, spirit plane guides, to those who remain. They try to help with thought and telepathic energy directed to those who will listen. Many times, when you are quiet, you will have thoughts come into your mind that are not yours at all. These thoughts are directed to you from some helper to enable you to understand something more completely.

Spirit plane helpers can also be those waiting for a return in an earthly body. It's not always that easy to return because so many are waiting in line. They have a short-term assignment to aid before they return. Or, helpers can be those who want and are able to assist those who remain in earthly bodies, for longer periods of time. They are not preparing for a return for some time, or at all. Helpers can also be assigned to different dimensions, such as the animal kingdom. Some helpers can be ones you have known from the distant past, some from the more recent past, and others known to you in your current life. Some have returned to the earth dimension many times, some very few. There are far more helpers than there are those incarnate on earth or elsewhere.

God, I have often been aware that certain thoughts weren't mine but were being sent to me telepathically. I try to listen and get help from what I'm hearing those in other planes share. I always know when it is *you* speaking to me. I can tell when it's an angel or helper; but I am not always sure immediately *who* is speaking until they tell me. Sometimes I can't hear clearly, and sometimes I think it's my imagination.

> That's right, Anne. Many people experience the same thing, although some feel they can't hear at all. Everyone who wants to hear can. Many don't want to. Here are all these spirit plane helpers that could aid everyone incarnate and few listen or believe. Yet, I have created this help. Most have forgotten the gift of telepathy and the many dimensions in which there is help besides the dimension in which you reside.

I heard a voice as I was meditating: "You have not forgotten the gift of telepathy. You are able to hear telepathically." Then the voice said, "Listen." and I heard voices from my left side enter into my left temple, like ticker tape, as friends and loved ones who had died spoke to me.

I talk with Stephen and my helpers a lot, as you know, but not to the extent I could because I get caught up in earthly things.

> Yes, and wouldn't it be magnificent to be caught up in *heavenly* things instead?

Yes. I will try to do better in this. More than anything else, I want to teach anyone who desires to, how to hear and talk with you and those in other dimensions.

> I have created many helpers and angels to work with you to help you, since each of you is in a different state of development while incarnate. Those in similar states of consciousness tend to group together. Those who group together and feel at odds, often return to less advanced or more advanced soul groupings to be more productive and comfortable. Everyone can hear me speak and those of you who are aware of this will want to teach others how to listen.

God I feel some intuitive things about my life, some remembrances that are vague, even some childhood memories. Are the things I perceive in dreams, meditations and attunement correct?

> You have had quite a number of experiences on earth; and, sometimes you grew from them, and sometimes you faltered. But, your growth was greater than your faltering, if you'd care to know. When it came time to decide to experience the earth dimension again, we had a long talk about it. You saw that choosing a female form would best suit you for the work you wanted to do and the lessons you wanted to learn. You reviewed your other experiences and made some decisions about what had caused your progress to slow and what had helped you grow. You set some goals, with my help, about how you would direct yourself in

the female form you were choosing. Then you met with some helpers who would aid you from their dimension after you had entered the female form. They would remain close to the earth, encouraging you and meeting with you. You planned some strategies to aid your growth. You were given some advice about maintaining the physical female form through understanding it as a body, mind, spirit and emotional vehicle.

Those are some of the remembrances I have had.

You were assigned other helpers, including angels; and, all this was before the parents conceived you. You checked out a number of couples to see where you would have the best conditions to do all you planned to do in the form you were choosing. You decided on the two who would create the best physical vehicle, and also the best early childhood experiences to prepare you for your mission. The situation wasn't ideal, as many aren't, but it turned out to be a good spiritual choice for you.

In a way you could think of it like buying a used car. You shop around for a good deal, you try to get the car that was taken care of best. You try to learn the history of the car; you check the interior, the exterior and try the motor or take it for a test drive. You see that it has some small problems or difficulties; but, you think you can handle them, since the motor seems to be in such good shape.

You and your helpers were aware of some of the problems or opportunities you might encounter, and probably would encounter. You decided that within your realm of choosing, this looked like the best choice. Besides, I had already told you that no matter how difficult an incarnation you might experience, that I would always be with you, and you could overcome and work effectively with anything. And, you believed me - then.

I guess I just forgot for awhile.

One little glitch you felt had to be looked into. The man who would be your biological father and help bring a strong physical vehicle into being - the female you - would not remain in your life from shortly after conception. Another would enter because of lessons he and your mother had to work through. So, you checked out the one who would raise you and found that his caring and kindness overcame other limitations.

You decided you were ready to return and things were set in motion. Remember I said there is no conception with a sperm and egg, unless there is *my* touch. Your call was for the spirit to touch the flesh, and I did, as I have done in all of creation. And you began this journey of your soul, which is neither male nor female, into awareness of this sojourn into the female form.

Your soul did not enter the form when I touched the flesh. It entered at my command when you took your first breath, as I have told you. As the form that would house your soul developed over the nine months, you and your helpers continued to plan the work ahead, often hovering around, observing the situations occurring in and around the family. Again, you were instructed in the earthly laws and possibilities, as is each soul, whether male or female.

Sometimes the group of you would gather around the one who would be your earth mother and send her thoughts. Some she heard, but many she ignored when awake. These were sent as thoughts about this child – you - that would enter, about her role, the child's mission and all those things of importance a parent should know and remember. These included suggestions about the ideal name for you, which she didn't remember. That's why you felt so drawn to change your name as you were growing up. The vibration of a name is far more important that many realize. When you stopped using your first name and went by your middle name, it was more in accord with your energies and life's work.

That's fascinating, God, about the name and all. It's also fascinating how we choose our parents.

In addition to you choosing the parents, the parents also agreed to their mission with you. When they were asleep or when their minds were elsewhere, we would all meet and discuss this venture. This is true for all souls entering and it is of great importance. The planning was made with all parties, including the father who would raise you, and even with the grandparents and relatives. It's a group effort, the entering of a child; and, it takes all of them to make a strong and whole incarnation. Often, many forget and make choices taking them way off track. The incoming child sees that it will lack enough support to thrive and fulfill what he or she came to do.

This would make the incarnation so difficult and ineffective for the growing child that, sometimes the pregnancy is terminated or a form is still-born. At times the child dies at an early age when it sees it can not accomplish what it came to do. There is a lot more to this, which I will tell you one day.

You chose a female form and this was in agreement with the group waiting for you and the group that would assist you. You began to be educated about how your role would be different from what would occur if you had chosen a male incarnation.

God could we take a break? I do want to hear all this, but I simply can't process any more right now.

Of course. I'm just delighted you are putting our talks and our relationship at a higher priority in your life.

God, I want to ask you about what happened last night. Herb and I were lying in bed together and both of us saw the bedside lamp come on by itself. The switch had been completely turned off. It had happened once before, some months ago. We began to question who was there. I heard Stephen and a spirit plane helper named Morton that I had talked with many times.

They said I had forgotten my experience with the group of writers from the spirit plane that had been assigned to me to do a special novel. I was told to begin to let them write through me for an hour a day. I hadn't followed their guidance given weeks before.

They also told Herb that Edgar Cayce would help him in his writing - to write each day and listen to him. They said not to get so wrapped up in other things that we don't write. Writing, they said firmly, is what we are to do and we must get about it.

> Well, Anne, what is your question? You seem to have gotten the answer.

How can those in other dimensions turn things off and on? Why didn't they just talk to us instead of turning on a light in the dark and surprising us? And, is their guidance true?

> Some of those in the spirit plane can use energy and thought to move things and turn electrical things off and on. Sometimes it's fun for them, and sometimes it drains their energy for days. In this case, they had fun. They got your attention, after trying for some time to talk to you. You heard correctly. Those who help with your writing will not do it for you; but aid you in getting certain helpful information out. Many so-called fictional novels contain truths that would not be accepted if written as non-fiction. These "fictional" accounts cause seeds of truth to be planted in many minds, to later help individual's growth into fuller awareness.
>
> Why should you be surprised about Edgar Cayce's help? I talked to him when he was in a physical body all the time as did angels and spirit plane helpers. You have talked with him for years. He still has an abiding interest in carrying on the work he began, through those few who will listen.
>
> Sometimes your helpers just want to get your atten-

tion, and have you listen to them. They have a great sense of humor, which is a spiritual gift. And, yes, the guidance they gave you is true.

– ✡ –

God, how can I possibly learn all I need to know this lifetime?

The key is remembering and applying. It's all there inside your memory bank in varying degrees. It is within each person, according to his or her past and present experiences. Anne, modern computers and the latest technology give us a better way to use analogies and metaphors than ever before. Computers are so easily compared with the mind and memory storage bank.

When you first get a computer and play solitaire to get used to it, you get better and win more and more. You soon tire of it, perhaps go on to other games, tire of the games, and go on to more useful and advanced programs. In life, this current lifetime, it is the same - you get better as you learn, practice and apply and you go on to other things. With computers you start off on some simple program, and then you become more confident in accessing your other programs. You begin to want more and more advanced software.

Some of the software gives you amazing tools and ways in which to work. Others take you to another step of expertise. You begin to see there is no end to technology. Some software must be studied diligently, actively applied and practiced with until you get better and better. With each step you get more confident and able to tackle even more complicated programs. You find unlimited resources you did not even know were available to you. People begin to ask you for help.

Your "computer memory bank," your hard drive, contains everything you have ever known, learned or experienced. It has all been saved. You access your programs, your sophisticated software, everything on your limitless hard drive, through meditation, listening, prayer, using telepathy, and various other ways. You teach others what you have learned.

Your memory bank is always state of the art, never obsolete, and is constantly being upgraded as you learn more and more.

MESSAGES FROM GOD

CHAPTER 4

…God talks about…
telepathy, intuition, dreams, and
communicating with the spirit plane…

God, would you explain what happened to me yesterday?

What don't you understand, Anne?

I was having computer problems and I couldn't figure out what to do. So I lay down to rest and I heard you say, "Go sit at your computer." I went to my computer and sat down to see what you were going to tell me. Instead, without thinking, I found myself picking up the phone and calling my friend Dennis. I dialed and before the phone rang, Dennis answered. He was calling me at the same moment! He helped me solve the computer problems. I know you had something to do with that, didn't you?

I did. You forgot that when you laid down, you said, "God, help me. Show me what to do." I knew your need and I spoke to you. You listened to me and I directed you to your computer, which is by your telephone. I put you in telepathic rapport with Dennis. I sent you the thought to call him. I knew he could help you. I sent him the thought to call you at the exact moment, so you would have no doubt that I am here helping you. Sometimes you need a little confirmation of that.

Thank you God. I was fried over the computer situation. That helped a lot.

You're welcome, Anne. However, for it to work as it did, there were a number of things that happened. Without each of them, this would not have worked so well. First, you had a need and took time to lie down and get quiet. Then you sincerely asked me for help. That's where most people stop and then think I don't answer. But, you listened to what I said, trusted my suggestion, and went to the computer to sit and wait for my next instruction. I then sent you the thought to call Dennis. You were not conscious of hearing it; but you followed this telepathic suggestion because you have gotten used to listening to me in different ways for so long. I sent the suggestion to Dennis to call you. He, too, followed this telepathic guidance, called and was able to help you solve the problem.

Now, teach every one who will listen to ask my help and then listen to my guidance. I speak in many ways: out loud, telepathically, through feelings, intuition and impressions, with visions, through others, and in dozens of ways. A good rule of thumb is to listen three times as much as you ask or pray. Most pray ten times

Chapter 4

> more than they listen, if they listen at all. Remind your brothers and sisters that I want to talk with them; and, remind them of my love and caring...even about computers.

I will God.

– ✡ –

God, is there any truth and helpfulness in astrology, numerology, tarot, or psychic guidance? How should we approach and evaluate this information?

> There is truth and helpfulness in all of these perspectives if worked with correctly. They can all have helpful aspects if done properly by someone with the correct spiritual motivation. If a person is drawn to giving counsel in any of these ways, and "giving counsel" is the correct term and way to use this guidance, they have almost always done this previously and sense its value. Giving perspectives that a truly seeking individual can study and sort out, and from which they can sieve out the gems of truth can be of aid and bring help and hope to them.
>
> If, on the other hand, an individual has previously worked with any of these tools to control, use undue influence over another, or just to fill their pockets monetarily, then their intent will influence and sometimes pollute the information. The intent of the one sharing the information, especially if they use it as a counseling tool to bring help to an individual, is the

greatest measure of whether the information is helpful and hopeful. All information should be given, received and worked with according to its helpfulness and hopefulness. It is accurate to the degree that it is helpful and hopeful.

It gives you a perspective on yourself?

Yes. Just as one would do research by reading, watching and searching out various perspectives on a subject, so too one should do such in getting perspectives about themselves. There is no greater research than understanding and knowing yourself. For to know yourself is to understand your strengths and weaknesses, and to make of your weaknesses strengths. To know yourself is to know me, to know and understand others better, and to love yourself and others more fully. The search for self-knowledge is always paramount in a life. Yet, many spend their lifetimes worrying about and putting their attention on others. They neglect the study of self.

To love yourself is not ego, but of absolute necessity in order to become all you are capable of being. For if you cannot love yourself, how can you truly love others. Without self-love, and knowledge of self on all levels, few can become their best or accomplish what they came to do.

Therefore, why not avail yourselves of many perspectives about yourself. Then decide for yourself whether the information can aid you in taking steps upward on your soul pathway. If guidance is given that causes you fear, or to doubt, simply say to yourself, "I refuse

> to accept that." Ask me and I will tell you if there is any truth or helpfulness in that particular guidance. In fact, ideally, before you seek such perspectives, bring to me your questions about working with a particular individual; and, I will direct you to those whose purposes are clear and whose ideals are in accord with your highest good.
>
> You can always come to me for guidance. Yet, do not think that I do not rest my spirit on others to bring help to you. One day you will know with a certainty that you can get all the answers you seek within yourself from me. It does not make you spiritually less evolved to seek perspectives from others. Just don't let any guidance limit you, cause you fear or doubt, or cause you to falter. Test all guidance with this question - "Is this helpful and hopeful and does it bring me closer to God and to my highest spiritual awareness." Is this enough of a sermon about your question?

Yes God, that's a very good sermon.

> Good, now what else would you ask me?

How does intuition work? Is there really such a thing as "mother's intuition" or a "woman's" intuition?

> By the nature of choosing a female form for this journey, things of the intuitive are often easier and seemingly more natural because of the many differences between men and women. Not that some men do not and can not have natural intuition to the same degree. Society currently has different expectations of females than males. From childhood males are treated and

programmed differently. That added to their specific hormones and other specific male characteristics, creates more of an effort for *most* men than for most women to trust their inner feelings.

A woman then, because of the link to her child, most often gets in rapport with it more fully than the male. Males that become caretakers of children find themselves more sensitive and aware like their female counterparts.

How does intuition work? Thoughts are broadcast like radio waves from every person all the time. Some signals are stronger than others; some are of greater and lesser intensity. Some are on different "wave lengths" or "frequencies." You are sensing thoughts from others all the time, every minute of every day. That is why you often feel something entirely different from what a person is saying. What you "feel" is generally more correct. You are all made up of energy. If you could see yourselves without the covering of the human form, you would see nothing but millions of rays of energy. They are like a moving tapestry flowing within the form. They are bound in part by it, but it also is flowing outside the form in every direction. That outward flow from each of you interacts with all others and you sense and feel things - thoughts, sometimes heat and cold, sometimes prickles of energy, other times movement or vibration.

This is part of what the aura is - that emanation from *inside* the form, that is visible as white light and color around the body. However, some of the aura is also energy directed *toward* the body, which are the prayers sent from another, that have not yet fully manifested in the form yet.

If your flow is moving correctly, and not stopped somewhere in the energy body, then you are more receptive to picking up the thought energy of another form, or many other forms. Energy gets stopped or bound for many reasons: emotions, faulty diet and elimination, pollution, incorrect choices from the present or past, imbalances of all kinds. The majority of people do not allow this flow as fully as they are capable. Therefore, they fail to receive telepathically or receive thoughts directed to them because of this blocked flow within themselves.

Also, many receive these on-going transmissions but doubt the telepathic information they receive. They have been taught to discount anything they can't hear with their ears, touch with their hands, see with their eyes.

Are telepathy and intuition the same thing?

Intuition is closely related to telepathy; but is more than simply thought transference. Intuition is also the processing through the eyes information not consciously seen, and experiencing smells that may not register consciously but impact on the sixth sense. Intuition is also hearing, feeling, touch, and telepathy, all processed through and influenced by the five senses. Therefore, some intuition is from the thoughts everyone is broadcasting, some from the other senses on levels of which the body and mind are not fully conscious.

> A mother senses things about her children and acts on this intuitive awareness. She can't easily explain how she "knew" or identify the source of the information. Sometimes it is referred to as "mother having eyes in back of her head" or explained by the woman as "I don't know how I knew, but I knew." Since women say and feel this frequently; and because it seems to happen so often between mothers and children, it is referred to as "women's intuition."

I remember feeling that way about my mother, and my children feeling that way about me.

> Many children are more aware of this ability of their mother than even the mother is aware. Also, much of the sixth sense or intuition is a carry-over from one's dreams. There is nothing that happens in your life that you don't first preview in your dreams. This includes marriages, births, deaths, things from the past and possibilities of the future, everything. You awaken with "feelings" which are usually ignored. If they were explored they would help you in the making of positive decisions for your journey toward greater understanding all your life.

> It is the rare person who records their remembered dreams, or if they record them, they seldom work with them. Therefore, so much helpfulness and insight is lost or not used fully during those 4-10 hours of sleep. Actually, what you call "sleep" is just a different level of consciousness where you and I talk more openly and freely. When you "sleep" you remember we are one, and nothing is hidden from you about yourself or others.

> It would be good for parents and children to share their dreams over the breakfast table. If the family studied their dreams and worked with them, by writing them down and reviewing them during the day, so much help could be given the child, and so much insight given the parents. There are whole tribes, of adults and children, that work together with their dreams each morning. In those tribes, which most would call "primitive," there is almost no crime or sexual exploitation, no jealousy or use of words and actions to hurt each other in other ways. Would not the benefits far outweigh the time it would take?

They would, God.

> If you will hear me, then, I will tell you again and again - *every dream is from me. Every* dream. Now when you record your dreams, ask me what the dream means and I will tell you. It will change forever how you look at and work with dreams and how helpful they are to you.

Why did I dream, recently, that a famous person took a gun and shot himself in the head?

> He had in fact taken a gun earlier in the day and was going to shoot himself in the head. He went to sleep, and planned to finish the job in the morning. You met with him in the spirit plane when both of you were out of your bodies. Your spiritual form was drawn to his need last night. You and other helpers interrupted this foolish plan, by counseling him. Pray for him. The remembered dream is a call to prayer. It is clarification to help you remember that you are out of the

body every night and many nights aiding those in need. Because Stephen took his own life, you are especially drawn to those who are suicidal and need help.

I had a dream about being in a body before, I know it was only a dream and probably symbolic but.....

> ...Only a dream, dear Anne. If you only knew - only a dream. Dreams are where your guard is down, all your expectations and prejudices are put aside, and you let me in. All of your dreams are me talking to you in a variety of ways. All of them. Every dream is a visit we have had together where I am sharing with you different things to help you know yourself and me.

But everyone who is a dream expert says differently.

> Well, who do you chose to believe?

You, God, but I have kept a dream journal for years and it means I need to go back and look at every dream to see what you were saying to me.

> You could do that - which would be very enlightening by the way, or you could commit to doing that with the next dream. Try it awhile and let me know what you think.

— ✡ —

I tried this the last few months and it's fascinating. I have often been unable to figure out what a dream meant. I was able to interpret each dream when I asked, "God, what is your message to me?"

> Yes, I thought you would find it so. What you're going to have trouble with is when I share something with you that you have been so programmed to feel differently about, and you start thinking this guidance is not from me.

I'll try not to do that.

> Good, because you will stop listening if you judge it that way. At least listen, then throughout the day, think about it, ask for inner guidance about it, then either discard it, or add it to your awareness.

— ✡ —

I have learned a lot from you today about myself.

> As you grow in wisdom and understanding, so will the wisdom you allow from me expand into your awareness. Anticipate that our visits will aid you and others in embracing life peacefully, in joy, without stress and doubt. Just aim for greater peace and joy and for more than 33% productivity and creativity.

Is 33% all I accomplished today?

> You did not accomplish that much. You did better than 1%, and 1% is better than nothing. Remember

that when you get discouraged. 100% is great, but 1% is better than nothing.

It must be hard to work with me. I'll try harder.

You have as long as it takes. You want everything to happen at once. You want closure on all issues *now*. Yet, I who created you, and need you and your help most of all will give you eternity to do what you think you must do.

You really only need to love. That's all. You do not need to write a book or even help one person if you don't want, although this would be good for your soul growth. Just love yourself and everyone and me. That's all. Just that. All the things you try to do to feel it's OK to occupy space on earth are illusions. There is just love. Nothing else. Just love. Be loving. For in being love, all else you desire will be added unto you.

I don't completely understand this, God, or how to do it.

You will.

God, I am less afraid to die than ever before in my life. Yet, I would like to live and enjoy the earth awhile longer. I do love so much of it here. I love having a body and a mind.

You will have as much time as you desire to stay in this body. How long would you like?

Oh, maybe at least 30 more years in good health.

> Then you will and can and shall, by following the spiritual, mental and physical laws that apply in the earth.

I can't imagine being that old. I don't want to be old and...

> Why do you think you must?

You mean I could be youthful at that age?

> Yes. Not artificially either. But, from the beauty within and the beauty without. You can be in perfect health. I will show you how. There are a few simple steps to put you or anyone in accord with the earthly laws. Adherence to these will extend your life and keep you as youthful looking and healthy as you chose. I will talk to you about those later.

> Good morning, Anne. See, I am you; but, I also am separate from you. Yet, we are one. You are beginning to understand.

Yes. I can feel that I'm one with you, and sometimes that I'm one with other people. I can't always maintain that feeling. You said you would explain how to have soul-to-soul contact with people; and also how to ask for protection for your loved ones and know they are watched over.

I briefly explained how your energy broadcasts constantly from within your energy form and through your earthly form to others. This helps you understand that you are sending energy at all times. Everyone and everything is picking up that broadcast to a greater or lesser degree. Now, imagine you have a garden hose, which is not connected to the faucet. When you turn on the water full force, it gushes out of the faucet at random, spraying on the ground, uncontrolled, in many directions. When you attach the hose to the faucet and turn it on, it comes out of the hose and can be easily directed wherever you want.

When you specifically ask to contact someone soul-to-soul with your mind and thoughts, it is much like attaching the hose to the faucet. Your thoughts can then be directed to another more fully, as you so desire. There is an automatic direction of thought when you think of an individual or situation. The thought goes directly to them and they receive that thought to the degree and intensity with which it is sent. In asking to contact someone soul-to-soul, you use your mind to direct that communication with greater focus, strength and power.

Here is a situation in which you might want to contact someone soul-to-soul. If you are having difficulty with a family member and know that words are to no avail, you can use this technique to communicate with them. You can begin by sending a loving and positive thought out to them, or praying for them. Then you simply direct this specific thought to them with your mind, "I ask to communicate with you (using their name is ideal) soul-to-soul. Then begin to talk to them telepathically, mentally, mind to mind, or speak out loud if you prefer. Tell them of your caring for them, of your concerns, of your love and desire to resolve whatever difficulties you have. Say whatever is in your heart. Know that they hear what you are sending, on a soul level, even if they aren't aware of it on a conscious level immediately. It matters not whether the person you are contacting is asleep or awake, quiet or working.

This is OK to do and won't interfere with their free will?

Be very careful not to use mind control when you do this. Never try to bend a person's will to your own. There is a fine line here. You want to help them understand how you feel, and resolve whatever difficulties you have; but, you do not want to do that by using your mind to control their mind.

When you have finished your communication to them, always pause and ask, "Is there anything you wish to share with me or tell me?" Then pause and listen to see if there is a telepathic message or impression you receive back from them.

This is an easy technique. It will take some practice for many to use this technique fully; but, it is spiritually very powerful and healing for both parties. By making a soul-to-soul contact, you bypass the conscious mind that puts up barriers. On the soul level there is rarely any barrier; but always the free will of the soul or individual is paramount. So, upon rare occasions the soul will not respond in a receptive way or allow healing to be sent.

You can sometimes see almost immediate results in resolving conflict. Other times it may take weeks or months for healing to occur. The soul-to-soul contact can be made daily and rarely needs to be done for more than fifteen minutes at a time, often less. In what you might term crisis situations, it could be done several times a day; other times once every few days or weekly.

This is a technique that enables parents of grown children to be of help no matter how distant or how old their children are.

God, is this what worked with a friend I suggested do this? He had four children. His wife had abducted them twenty years before. He hadn't seen them since.

Yes. You suggested he ask to contact each of his children by name, daily, tell them of his love for them, ask them to find some way to contact him, and explain to them what had happened. One of them contacted him after three months of his prayers and soul-to-soul contacts. They now all visit and he has become acquainted with his grandchildren. It really works. It is how I have created you to use the powers of your mind and spirit. In the spirit plane, which you call "death," telepathy is the form of communication. It's good to practice communicating in this way and makes communication easier when you return to that plane.

What about doing this if a child is kidnapped or missing? Would it work then?

This is one of the most helpful and comforting things a parent can do in such a case. They can make the soul contact, speak to the child, comfort them, and tell them everyone is searching for them. Then they can ask the child to communicate back. If they will work with this, they will be able to sense how the child is; and, sometimes be comforted that the child is safe and not being harmed. Other times they will know that the soul of the child has released from the body and is at peace and free from any trauma. While this can be heartbreaking, it can also be comforting. There are parents who have done this and shared their experiences with others.

This method is also a peaceful way to keep in contact with and help protect your loved ones when they are away from you, even when there is no known difficulty to be concerned about. Dialogue with them daily. When they are away at college, for instance, keep in touch soul-to-soul. You can tell them that you are asking me to send angels to surround them from any negativity, and to protect them from harm. I will most certainly do that, if you but ask. I have bands of angels that need assignments. The spiritual laws involving them require you to call upon them to help, or to ask me to send them to your loved ones. I will always do this when you ask. This surrounds them with powerful energy that pushes away harm and negativity. It also creates within you deep inner peace. You don't have to worry about them. You know that they are in my watch-care.

A mother told me one of her children wouldn't speak to her and kept her grandchild away from her. I suggested she use this technique daily and ask the protection of your angels for them both. I suggested she also ask to meet them both in her dreams each night, and ask to be allowed to play with her grandchild nightly. She told me later that she would wake up each morning, feeling peaceful and comforted. After a time the situation was resolved lovingly.

> She did well. This is, again, how I have created all of you to interact with each other. Not just physically, verbally and emotionally, but spiritually - soul-to-soul. So few remember or avail themselves of this help.

This technique has helped me for years ever since you told me this. This same mother said that she would often remember dreams about her child and grandchild the next morning.

> These dreams were residues of actual visits they had all had together. Remember, I told you that all dreams are messages from me. The messages in her dreams were that I showed her she actually had met with her loved ones, because of her prayers and asking to be with them.

What an amazing thing, God. Most people have no idea they can do this and what a comfort it would be.

> They have just forgotten. We will remind them.

> It is also ideal to talk telepathically to newborns and young children. They will be able to tell you their needs; and, it will be of great help to them in not feeling so trapped in an earthly form until they are able to talk and move around more freely. Every child, from birth, hears and is aware of every conversation and comment uttered within their range of hearing, and

Chapter 4

far beyond that. It is all stored in their memory bank. They are also aware of the thoughts and feelings of the people around them. It is very important to monitor what goes on within their hearing and seeing, because they soak it all up like a sponge.

When you have a concern about one of your children, put a photo on the refrigerator or where you see it every day, and pray for them. Ask to meet in the Dream State and talk to them soul-to-soul frequently. Prayer is such a powerful gift to give to anyone. You know how stressed you feel sometimes? Your children often feel a thousand times worse. They are often filled with self-hatred, are unwilling yet to learn, and struggle in the darkness of addictions, fears and guilt. Surrender them to me for healing, even as you continue to pray and do these things. Declare them whole and healed.

Also, parents, especially mothers, are so deeply linked to their children that they feel their fear and pain. Yet, most know they must let them work things out, even while setting guidelines and lovingly enforcing those guidelines. Parents agonize over it while their children learn. They watch their children painfully experience their incorrect choices rather than learn in easier ways.

It's very similar to a puppy. You know he must get trained and learn better habits, yet you can't stand to see him suffer. You feel guilty and you postpone and prolong his training. He continues with his bad habits, sometimes to his own detriment.

Yes. I see that.

> Anne, you, like many parents and grandparents, are fearful of the pain you feel when your children hurt. You are fearful of their pain *and* of your own.

Yes, I guess I am.

> Don't be fearful. What do you have to fear? I am with you, and with them. If you will have faith and take all things one step at a time, it will all be done, and unfold as it should. I can help make it much easier for you. Just ask me. I have so much help to give, so much to share. Most of you don't even bother asking my help. You know how much wisdom you feel you have to share with your children, and they either don't want to hear or ignore your advice. Listening to and following your advice would save them many heartaches, and make their pathway much easier. It's not so different with my suggestions.

Yes, I can relate to that, God. When I ask you how to help or what to do for someone I care about, and follow what you say, it is always correct and helpful. Working this way with you could be comforting and helpful and much easier for so many others too.

> Yes, Anne, very much so. But, people have mostly forgotten all these gifts available to them. They have forgotten that I created them to talk with me daily. They have forgotten that my watch-care and protection is far stronger than any burglar system, can of pepper spray or other methods of seeming safety.

I used these suggestions in working with one of my children who was having problems. It really helped. I continue to work this way frequently with family and friends.

Have faith that it will always help. Persevere and don't doubt. Affirm the goodness of the person you are contacting, both to them and to yourself. For, there is good in all. Sometimes you just have to hose off a few layers to get to that visible goodness.

Now, let's talk about Heaven and Hell and the other myths that cause such chaos.

Heaven and Hell. Those are sensitive issues for people.

Do you really think I would let any of my creation be destroyed? And, what kind of creator would cause those who don't follow my supposed arbitrary rules to be burned in eternal fire? Not *ME*. I created all of you to succeed and I will help you as long as it takes -

throughout the eternities. I will never give up on you. You have free will to do whatever you want, for as long as you want, as much as you want. I will walk beside you until you remember who you are, who we are, and are ready for a helping hand.

There is no Heaven, there is no Hell, and there is no purgatory, as such. There are dimensions of experience that you are drawn to until you are ready for a lighter, higher dimension. But, I do not send you there nor keep you there. The moment you desire to be somewhere else, to grow in awareness, in that instant you move to a different level of experience.

Death is not to be feared, but embraced. It is the next door to go through after the earthly door. Death will be what you expect it to be until you are ready to realize it is a blessing not a curse. It is a next step, a new open door, a beginning not an ending, a return to awareness of me, of oneness with me. Fear not death; fear only that you will not use moments of experience for the fullness of joy.

People don't like the word "psychic." I don't like the word either, God.

Psychic is of the soul. It is an attribute of your soul, a gift of your spirit. Jesus was one of the greatest psychics of all time. Would you not desire to be like him? He had no hesitation in using his gifts. All great souls, like Jesus, are psychic, meaning that they use their *soul* abilities more fully than most. Yet, everyone is psychic and has many gifts that go unused. None of you should fear your abilities, nor fear calling them psychic gifts. Use those special gifts to grow and to help others. Develop gifts of intuition, of even sensing the future. Develop gifts of touch as in psychometry, of feeling as in sensing individuals needs, pains and strengths.

Use the gifts of healing you are each endowed with. For healing comes simply from believing that all healing is from me and can be directed through you to another. No one is a healer; but all can heal, if they believe they can aid another in this way. Use your gifts of attunement to talk with me, with the angels, with your helpers and with those who no longer use physical forms. All who truly desire can do this. It is neither dangerous nor to be feared. All these gifts are your birthright if you will but claim them. And all of these gifts are psychic gifts, gifts of the soul.

If you want other words you are more comfortable with, try Spiritual Counselor, Sensitive, Mystic or Christian Mystic. However, don't throw the word "psychic" away because some few misunderstand or are ignorant of its real meaning.

Why is it God that we seem to be able to use these gifts and do these things better for others than ourselves?

You don't. You have bought into a powerful thought form that tells you this, and it is not true. You are always your own best psychic, sensitive, healer, intuitive. Always. Others can be catalysts, but ultimately only you can make it all work together for your good. This is the power I have endowed you with.

But it often doesn't work.

Because you approach it in such a limited way. You approach the mind, or you tend too much to the body, or you think spiritual laws are all there are. There are laws governing the body, mind and spirit. One cannot be whole without the three in accord and harmony. In the use and application of all these gifts within yourself or in helping another, there must be the attention to all three. You must discover the laws that govern each. Work with these laws, and in doing so, you can create balance and harmony in all things.

God, how can I possibly learn all these things, these laws, and apply them and have any other life?

This *is* your life, Anne. These things are life. The rest is clutter.

So we're back to clutter?

Yes, cluttering the mind with all sorts of things causes such delay in the progress of your soul. What most people put in their minds creates a garbage dump and sewer-filled consciousness. Clutter of the body creates illness. It is equivalent to a bathroom overflowing with backed up plumbing. That's why you should drink large quantities of water at specific times of the day, to flush clutter out of the body. Clutter of the mind with

> thousands of bits of misinformation, misconceptions and religious dogma is like being held captive under thousands of pounds of rocks and material objects, unable to move and barely able to breathe.
>
> Simplifying is correct. Simplify things within the house and your life. Clutter around you adds to the clutter within you. Clutter. I like that word because it sounds like what it is. Clutter! Imagine you have a clutter-remover. Make it a bulldozer, a roto-rooter, or a fire hose, digging and flushing out clutter. Imagine with all the clutter removed what good that might enter those cleaned out spaces.

God, it sounded like you laughed.

> I did. God laughs. All god-beings should laugh often; it is a great clutter remover and spirit lifter.

Why is it so hard to forgive? Is there some way to really forgive people?

> You must forgive everyone someday. Now is a good time. Be honest but fair, and be loving. Make a list of everyone you need to forgive, then forgive them fully. In your mind and prayers say, "I forgive you and I forgive myself, and you are free and I am free. I do this in my name and in the name and healing power of my Creator, now and for all the eternities.

> It is true for you and for most that there is still a lot of pain from all the people who have hurt you during your life. You neither want nor need most of them back in your life. Things are much better and you are growing at a much deeper spiritual level this way. Always release them to their own devices with love. Care not what matter of evil they may have done or said about you. Care only that you keep your slate clean of anger or criticism. Release them to me. Do not defend yourself. Do not care. They have mistakenly judged you on their 1% perception of you. Pray for them or send them to me for healing. Then you are free to grow. Your lessons with them are over. You have no further need for them in your life.

I finally understand what you meant when you said, "Judge not that ye be not judged."

> Good.

— ✡ —

God, could you please check and be sure that every word of your messages are as you would have them?

> Good morning Anne. All these years you have heard me. You have heard from others in their dimensions, too, and you have often doubted. I see that your doubt has eased somewhat. But, you have felt me there whispering in your ear as you received the guidance you asked me for. You have heard me as I guided you to make these messages understandable. I will continue

to direct your thinking. We will talk, as we are now, whenever you desire; and, we will work on this together. Remember this book is already written; it is already a fact, created by your mind and thoughts with my direction. It is complete, the goal is reached; now, all you need do is walk toward the peak and carry it with you.

It's complete already? That takes a lot of pressure off.

With each word I will be here and help you. You have chosen to co-create with me. I will do my part even as you are doing yours. See it's the little things that get you caught up and off the track. Stick to writing and listening to me and it will work fine. Put everything else on the shelf temporarily.

Here's a simple and effective way to learn to focus and get things done. Put all the things you feel you need to do in boxes in your mind. Separate each thing into its own box. Place the boxes, lids closed but unsealed, on a shelf. Set priorities, of which box is to be done first, which second and so on. Take down one at a time. Work on the contents of that particular box. When you start thinking about the contents in another box and reach for it, put it back until you are finished with the box on which you are working.

Again and again your mind will try to remove other boxes from the shelf. Each time put the boxes back. Tell yourself that you will take that next box down after you are finished with the current one. Keep doing this until all the boxes except the one you are working on remain on the shelf. Devote yourself to only one box at a time. Finish one box before opening another. A few hours or days or weeks delay in opening another box will not hurt. It will help you immensely in getting what you want to accomplish completed.

You might call this compartmentalizing, or setting priorities. The visualization of the boxes and the shelf will simply enable you to become more productive and finish any project you start.

You can even make an actual shelf with little boxes with labels on them of the things you want to accomplish.

I tried this God. It works! I saw in my mind the boxes and shelf each time. I must have put boxes back on the shelf a hundred times. Finally, they stayed there. Then I actually made a dozen or more boxes and labeled them. I have never gotten more done.

I can hear you and your messages inspire me; but I procrastinate and am so far from enlightenment and awareness. Why is this so?

It is lack of faith, Anne.

Lack of faith? What does faith have to do with it?

Lack of faith creates fear. You became fearful of lack, of want, of outcomes, of almost everything. You lack faith to believe you can have and be anything you choose. You fear so much, especially lack. This is

> from childhood. You chose to come in to learn what it means to seemingly have lack and then overcome it. You came to learn how difficult it is for people to do what they say they will do, so that you would stop being judgmental. You are learning, somewhat slower than you had planned; but you have made progress.

I thought I had a lot of faith.

> Anne, there are many lessons. As you grow, and learn certain lessons, others move to the front of the line to be dealt with. Those you have learned become the foundation for your soul growth. What a great way to grow. Remember that - no trials and tribulations, no tests, just learning and growth.
>
> Even though you can't quite understand how it's possible, I am always here. You don't need to wait for me or wonder if I'm with you. I am never *not* with you. Never. I have been with you for each breath you have taken, I have heard your first word, watched your first kiss, comforted your first pain, heard you cry from hunger as a newborn, heard you cry from sadness at your first broken love affair. I have joyed in each moment of your creation, and I have spoken to you always.

That makes me cry. It also makes me feel very loved and cared for.

> You are. Now care for yourself, and let me care for you as you learn. Together we will create your health, wealth and happiness. Don't be so hard on yourself; yet, be harder on yourself than anyone else will ever

be on you. Don't faint and sit down on the pathway before the race is finished. Above all, don't let discouragement, fear and doubt erode away your confidence and joy. Call them whatever you will - the devil's tools, the rocks on the pathway that cause you to falter, the evils of the world. But call them something! Fear and doubt are the enemies standing between you and a joyous lifelong journey. Eliminating them makes your faith grow.

Anne, there may always be some valleys; but, while you may walk in them for awhile, they do not go on forever. Climb always the mountains for the better view and to strengthen you. For, the valleys will be inviting; but you cannot see clearly in the valleys, only from the mountaintops. The valleys can strengthen you, as do the mountains; but, welcome the climb, for it is in the climb that you grow. It is on the summit that you observe that growth. When you reach the mountaintop, you will also see other mountains waiting to be climbed. You will see what the future holds.

So, embrace change and transform stress into productivity. You can't do it all at once. You can do it a step at a time. I will direct your footsteps if you will so allow.

Life can be such a wonderful adventure for you! Enjoy the journey!

MESSAGES FROM GOD

CHAPTER 5

...guidance from God about...
earthly laws governing health, weight,
and the secrets of staying young....

God, there are a thousand books on what you should and shouldn't eat. Is there an ideal diet for everyone?

> There are earthly laws governing what keeps human life form in the best possible health for the longest life span. These laws, if followed, assure health and longevity, and a life of harmony and joy. Here are some of them.
>
> Eat foods filled with the life force, grown near where you live, as fresh from a garden as possible, and eaten soon after being harvested. That is the way foods contain the most nutrients and still have the greatest life

force in them. Have a garden, too, if you can, and work it yourselves. Start a compost pile, using garbage that you would ordinarily throw out. It helps the soil and the environment.

What if you live in an apartment and can't have a garden, or don't have time?

In apartments you can plant herb gardens, do sprouting and grow a few things in pots on a patio or in windowsills. Your number one priority is to take care of your health. Without good health much else in your life never gets done. Your health is definitely a higher priority than television, for instance. Eat organic foods when possible, or foods without pesticides on them. Eat regular meals so that you do not choose foods in a rush that aren't health building, to satisfy your hunger.

Do not eat when you are stressed or rushed. Wait until you are calm. This alone will help you to absorb a greater amount of nutrients from the foods you eat. If you eat when you are stressed or distraught, the body does not process the food correctly and you do not absorb the nutrients from the foods as fully. Many times foods eaten under these conditions actually make you sick. Eating when you are rushed also causes you to eat too rapidly, instead of chewing your food slowly. Your adrenal and thyroid glands begin to malfunction. Eventually you develop allergic reactions to foods that are usually health building. Soon most everything you eat begins to make you feel bad. The cycle repeats itself.

What about water and juices?

Drink 8-10 large glasses of water a day. Drink a glass a half-hour before each meal, a glass two and a half to three hours after each meal, a glass upon awakening, a glass before bed. Drink fresh vegetable and fruit juices. Eat and drink more vegetables than fruit and do not take them together for they are not assimilated well in combination. Foods and drinks purchased from fast food places and eaten in restaurants contain so much fat, additives and salt as to cause the body to hold, not release weight, as well as to make the body extremely toxic over a period of time. They are not ideal fuels for human life forms.

A healthier eating program, where you have control of how food is gathered and prepared is one of the answers. Eating and drinking more slowly, chewing fully, and making eating a holy sacrament is another answer. Know that your body is a sacred temple that temporarily houses your soul. Eating several balanced meals in moderation is better than gluttony. The body eats rapidly and overeats when its nutritional needs are not met. Foods don't always contain enough nutrients, because of how they were grown and handled, or from staying on the grocery shelves too long. One craves more food when the quality of food is lacking. Smelling and breathing in aromas of what you are eating, and chewing and eating slowly helps greatly.

Some of these things aren't possible for many people, God.

That's right, but almost everyone can do better than the way they are choosing to eat. Those with limited income will actually eat far better and cheaper with the suggestions I am giving you. Many cities have farmer's markets, grocery stores that stock organic vegetables and fruits and even traditional stores that carry nutritious foods if you are careful in your selection. The foods that are not health building are far more expensive than those are that will bring you energy and extend your life.

Is a strictly vegetarian diet the best?

Many purists will also not like this truth: meat in moderation is not harmful. Eating of meat, fish and fowl do not make you less spiritual, or less healthy, nor do you automatically eliminate them when you become more enlightened.

But many experts say meat is toxic and that dairy products should be eliminated.

We created all things to sustain life on this earth. Therefore, almost all growing things used wisely can sustain life. Those that aren't edible can be used for healing and made into various products to aid. An ideal diet would be 75% grains, seeds, legumes, vegetables, and fruits, with an abundance of water. The other 25% can be meats, fish, fowl, milk (yes, milk), butter, yogurt, oils, honey and various things that are not overly processed nor added to.

Anything chemical and processed does not contain the life force. Raw vegetables, fruits, seeds and nuts do contain the life force if grown and handled correctly. Even lightly cooked foods contain the life force to a lesser degree, and minimum cooking benefits through its calming effect to the body. Chemicals and processing are not in harmony with health and longevity.

Well, there are many times I am also stressed and agitated and don't know why. Is this because of eating incorrectly?

Sometimes, yes. The laws governing the physical body in your dimension, if followed bring health and vitality, as I have shown you. You rebel against these very laws. They are not meant to restrict or limit, but bring greater strength and peace.

First, one of the laws governing the physical body: drinking eight or more glasses of water daily will flush toxins from your body and hydrate your entire system. Drinking water with meals will not hurt you, despite what you have been taught. Throw that incorrect information away.

Secondly, eating living foods in any quantities will balance the body and add to vitality and energy. Eat fruits, unprocessed nuts and seeds, even grains, vegetables of all kinds, not worrying whether they have a high fat content. Olive oil and milk products such as yogurt can be used in moderation. Almost anything that lives and grows in nature is life-building and healing. Consume vegetables and fruits without any restrictions. Meat won't hurt you in small amounts if it is not filled with pollutants and hormones. No meat whatsoever will also be fine for those who so choose, using legumes and other proteins instead. Occasional fish, chicken, turkey or lamb can also be eaten, but make these a very low percentage of the diet.

Many things in moderate amounts are not harmful, such as butter, whole grain breads, brown rice, eggs; but most don't understand moderation. Eat mainly those things which contain the life force, and have no pollutants or sprays on them. Vegetables and fruits should not be cooked for the most part, but when cooked, baked or steamed lightly with fresh herbs. Use salad dressings made without such unhealthy additives. Snack on vegetables with a vegetable dip at times, and eat all you want. After awhile you will not want so much. You will see your entire health transformed and your stress and agitation will disappear. This is true for most.

Some of these things you are sharing, God, are what different experts promote, others are in opposition with many of them. I am willing to throw out old preconceived notions I have about diet and health. Can you tell me other things that will help?

Artificial sweeteners of every kind are foreign to all bodies, and a slow poison. Sugar is poison too, except for unprocessed sugar cane. Food dyes, additives, those things to prolong shelf life are foreign to the body. Candy, sugars, desserts, processed foods and all these unholy concoctions do not feed the body anything of value. Honey, dates, unprocessed nuts and seeds, date sugar or molasses are health building, despite what you might read, and would be better for long-range sustained energy. The key is returning to nature to eat and be healthy. This means not eating out where you can not so easily control what you eat and when you are unable to eat healthfully. This is the healthy, life-extending way to fuel your body, and to be in accord with the physical laws governing it. Everything that goes into the body that is not health-building is health destroying and life-shortening ultimately.

Aren't we pretty safe if we eat and drink everything in moderation?

Many people have lived by that rule. However, it is not ideal because those things that I just mentioned, and others, are not good even in moderation.

If everyone understood this and ate in the healthier way according to the earthly laws, no one would need vitamin therapy, or very little. Illness would be almost totally eradicated. Vitamins and minerals can aid greatly while restoring balance, but are rarely needed by a healthy body. Fasting at times from a meal, for a day, or a week cleanses the body, and is far better than any colonics or enemas, although these can be helpful to detoxify your system at times. Use pure water and fresh vegetable or fruit juices when fasting, or just water. Never fast from water, ever. Water is what keeps you alive.

If you want to live this life in perfect health, return to the basics. It would help heal the planet if everyone did. Declutter your body and then declutter your planet. Feeding of cattle, the pollution of the environment from the animals, all this destroys the planet. Raising of most kinds of animals to eat is not the best use of the land. Growing of natural crops is. The reason you and others crave so much and overeat, whether you are overweight or not, is because the vegetables and fruits grown and sprayed excessively do not smell or taste the ways that would satisfy your needs. An apple that has little odor and taste, causes you to crave several more apples to get the satisfaction that one apple grown correctly would. Or it causes you to stop eating the tasteless food and sets up cravings in your mind and body for what is lacking.

Over-processed, fried and fast foods get you used to tastes that cause you to crave more. They do not satisfy you and cause eating disorders such as anorexia and obesity, loss of energy and health and extreme cravings for additional food of that type, as well as contributing greatly to other addictions. In a short time the major fast foods corporations could clean up their menus to a great extent, and add to the health and vitality of the world.

Eating, preparing food, serving food, even shopping for food is a holy experience and should be considered so. For you are feeding the temple in which you reside so that your soul can do the work it came to do. If you are preparing food for others, consider it a sacred service for them. Do it with love, for the very food you prepare for yourself and others is altered in a positive or negative way by your thoughts while preparing it.

This takes a lot of time and energy when most of us have careers and families.

Let part of your work be in healing your families through preparing and selecting life giving foods, and being the example, without preaching. This is something women and men càn do to make a difference in the world. You feel you don't have enough time, yet you will find time to take care of yourself and others when they become ill.

Many people try to medicate themselves and handle stress with food, alcohol and other substances, instead of coming to me for the peace they seek. What they are truly seeking is the oneness with me that they have forgotten but what their soul longs for. The longing for me cannot be satisfied by these things which they substitute.

Also, being active, through exercise that you enjoy, adds to the strengthening of your holy temples, and helps lengthen your life span. Weight lifting appeals to some, running to some, and bicycling to others. Do not let them become addictions. Walking is the best of all movement exercises. You have heard this from many sources, and it is true, Walking can aid greatly in healing. So a combination of commitment and perspiration creates results.

Or you could say commitment and perseverance creates results, too, couldn't you?

Yes, I just thought that commitment and perspiration painted a pretty accurate picture.

It does. Why don't we all just *do* it? Why do we suffer unnecessarily?

On this planet, as you see with many, it is easier to take a pill, be on medication, or rely on someone other than yourself for your health. The individual and group health on your planet is atrocious. People die well

> before their minds or physical bodies wear out. They suffer untold agonies to the body and mind when it is all preventable. I did not create disease and suffering to help you learn lessons. That is one of the worst lies about me. I created you to live in joy and learn in joy. Remember that. Suffering does not please me, sacrifice does not please me, and pain does not please me. Of course you can learn lessons from illness and pain, but why do it the hard way?

It feels as though a lot of what I have read and believed may not be true and I need to really look into some things more clearly, and not be limited by old incorrect beliefs.

> Yes, and ask me and I will guide you when you seek truth or when there is confusion.

What about emotions and eating?

> There is, of course, the emotional element, since the mind, body and spirit are totally interconnected; and there is the spiritual element. Many snack to calm the nerves when they are better calmed through meditation, inspirational reading and being out of doors and walking or having creative activities. Snacking on foods without life force is an endless loop. The more you snack, the more you crave. Snacking on living foods can be calming to the emotions.
>
> As I told you, many use food, drink and drugs to ease the pain they feel from their separation from me. Overeating, addictions and the taking of various substances are but a form of slow suicide, because of a

lack of awareness of my love and of our oneness. It is an effort to stop the pain of what they perceive to be our separation. They have just forgotten. These substances may create a temporary feeling of peace, or even forgetfulness, but it does not last. The spiritual oneness between us cannot be found except by remembering who you are and by claiming our ultimate attunement together.

You mentioned to me about "fueling" the body. Will you explain more about that?

Think of your body as an expensive car needing the proper fuel. The right fuel in your body makes such a difference in your health, your attitude and energy as well as your desire to help others. The human form was created to respond with vitality and health to the proper fuel put into it through a process of assimilation and elimination. It resonates powerfully to the vibrations of those things put into it that contain the life force. The body was also created to be kept flexible through activity. It was created to be peaceful through correct breathing, meditation and attunement with me.

Everyone has a theory about diet, exercise and longevity. Optimum health is really very simple. Stay in harmony with the earthly laws governing the physical body and you will never be ill. You will live far longer than the current earthly life span. Even certain environmental pollution and various other things beyond your immediate control will not have the same adverse effects if you stay in harmony.

How would you define good health, God?

> Most people have adapted so well to poor health that they are no longer aware of what good health is. Good health is to be at peace body, mind and spirit and to be in harmony, filled with joy. It is to be able to be fully functional physically and mentally at every age. Good health allows you to move with freedom, have an active and seeking mind and a desire to help others in various ways. A truly healthy person is filled with hope, enthusiasm and zest for life no matter what age. Good health is being able to do the good things you want with your body, mind and spirit and welcome change and new experiences with the joy of a child. Good health enables you do let go of all limitations and use each moment of life fully.

God, is there some secret about losing weight? If so, lots of us would like to know what it is.

> Let's talk about that. Losing excess weight isn't just about cutting down on food. Almost everyone you know could eat less and more wisely, excess weight or not. Releasing unwanted weight is understanding that you are not just a body, you are also a mind and a spirit, and each of those parts of you need to be taken care of. For they are dimensions of the total you. Proper food, exercise, peaceful thoughts, helpful and inspiring reading material, rest, relaxation, helping others, enthusiasm for life, friendships, someone to share

your thoughts and plans with, making love even, are important. The key is total balance.

See yourself as three beings in one. If the physical body is sick, it affects the mental body, making it unable to stay clear and functioning. This affects the spiritual body, making it feel discouraged, losing hope, lacking enthusiasm for life. If the mental body is out of accord, you know how it affects the physical body, and this seems the easiest for people to understand. Almost none comprehend how the mind and body affect the spirit, or how the spirit affects them.

You get to know yourself and your needs through understanding your physical, mental and spiritual needs. Then you make the changes and corrections to bring your three selves into harmony. The healing process is different for each individual; but being in accord creates wholeness with the earthly laws affecting the physical, mental and spiritual.

When, for instance, you eat according to the laws governing the physical body for the ideal maintaining and care of the physical form, you do not eat in excess. Excessive intake of food and drink is simply because a body is not receiving the nutrients it needs. The body is suffering from malnutrition. It will continue to take in excessively trying to satisfy that need. Eating foods containing the life force, as given, brings the balance to excess or even inadequate body weight.

That makes sense, but knowing what to do and doing it are two different things. How may we get ourselves to *do* what we know is best to do?

That's where I come in. I can't do it for you. Remember that you always have free will to choose to do or not to do something. I can, however, suggest when you ask my help. I can give you the strength you need moment by moment. I can also send others to help you, both those in the earth plane and those in the spirit planes.

For example, if you are shopping in a grocery store, you can ask before selecting a particular vegetable if it is still filled with nutrients or of any nutritional value. You can ask about any food as to whether it is good for your body.

You mean stand at the vegetable counter and ask about everything before you buy it? That would take forever.

No, it won't take forever. As you work in this way more and more and trust my guidance, you will be able to ask or know almost instantaneously what is health building and what is not for you. That is the ideal way. I will send you a thought, or a helper will bring you the answer you are seeking. Always. Just ask, listen and trust; then act on that guidance.

That's all there is to it?

No, there is more. When you sit down to eat a meal, pick up something to snack on, dine at someone's home, or eat out in a restaurant, do the same thing. Ask if a particular food is correct for you at this time. You will be given the answer. Leave it on your plate and don't eat the food if the answer is "no." However, don't think that if a food isn't correct for you at that time that it will never be ideal to eat. Sometimes, because of your physical or emotional state, a food would be toxic for your system for a day or more. Later your body may assimilate it quite well. Other times there could be something wrong with the way it is prepared or it may contain pesticides or other things, which are not health building.

You begin to take control of your physical body and you eat only those things, which strengthen and empower you. Most people eat un-consciously, without thinking. Balance and harmony to the body come from conscious eating.

Instead of dieting, since the word has such failure connotations, think of health building and substituting.

Substituting what?

Healthier foods for junk food. Substitute exercises that are fun for lying around watching television. Substitute positive thoughts for negative ones, love for hatred, water for sodas, prayer for others instead of worrying about self. Substitute gardening, art, reading, or whatever you would love to do, for eating.

To motivate yourself more fully, carry around a backpack that is filled with something that weighs the amount you need to release. Try it for a day or longer. You will clearly see that your body has adapted to this extra load but it creates great wear and tear on the entire body, mind and spirit.

More and more obesity will be a paramount issue in

the lives of children and adults, as much of humankind becomes more sedentary and consumes food with no life force. In years to come, as is true now, there will be the searching for a miracle drug, diet or cure for excess weight. The only "secret" is to eat health-building foods, hydrate the body cells, be more active and bring the body, mind and spirit into balance.

In releasing excess weight, which does not serve you, you may step by step reverse the way in which the weight was gained. Think about that and you will see what I mean.

Something confuses me, God. I always thought I should only ask you to help with major things of great importance in my life, and not bother you for minor things. How can you possibly have time to answer every question everyone and I would have about every bite we would eat?

There are two errors in this thinking, Anne. One is in believing that I am not interested and involved in *everything* in your life. I am aware of each breath you take, of each thought you think and of everything you do. There is no moment, no space, no time when I am not totally aware of you in every way. Secondly, remember I told you that the laws governing my dimension allow me to be everywhere at all times. So I am not limited in the help I can give one person or millions. Also, questions about the proper fuel needed for your physical body and optimum health are not minor questions. Without health you cannot get as much of your life purpose accomplished.

I can hardly comprehend your caring and help for the whole world.

> Just to exercise your mind some more, try: "for the whole universe."

You can do that for the billions of people in the world and all the souls in the universe?

> Yes, even those in all the *universes*.

That really blows my mind. How many souls are there in the universes?

> More than you can comprehend in numbers.

Oh. Then we are not the only intelligent life in the universe?

> No, of course not. We'll talk about that some other time.

You said we could talk about illness and how to cure disease. Is this a good time?

> Of course. So many diseases and ailments just need the body to rest for a few minutes, a few hours, or a few days or weeks. Many women feel they don't dare rest, as if somehow it is not productive and they must

be "doing" all the time. Where does that come from? It comes from advertising, books written without a true awareness of the need for spiritual attunement time, and the false notion that they need to excel in everything. It comes from many other things too. Women then create maladies to rest: colds, stomach upsets, flu, exhaustion, depression, whatever it takes to lie down awhile without feeling guilty. If that doesn't work, you create more severe illnesses and even accidents, when all you need is to give yourself permission to rest.

For men it is not much different. Many men won't overtly rest, but they can watch sports so they don't feel as guilty for sitting down and relaxing. Men create more serious diseases to rest. Heart attacks, major things. Their guilt is greater, and their inability to allow themselves to express emotions and feelings adds to their stress. Many men and women feel such guilt for needing rest and time for themselves that this immobilizes them. By not allowing time for these basic needs, they become of little help to themselves or the ones who need them most.

It sounds so simple.

It is simple. Here are some other suggestions. When you are tired, rest, when you are hungry eat, when you are thirsty drink, when you are sad cry, when you are happy laugh, when you are confused pause and pray, when you are joyful stand up and proclaim it. When you are feeling the need to do something, unless it hurts another, do it. And do it without guilt. You will find your other hours much more productive.

What can we do to change this, God?

> Humans have been so programmed to do so many things, which are against their nature, that much deprogramming is needed. It is not natural to push yourself beyond endurance instead of resting; and it will exhaust and wear out the physical form more quickly. Neither is lying around doing nothing day after day health building. It is natural to work a little, play a little, rest a little, cry a little, laugh a lot, and read a little. This is the way humans were created to last and endure longer than they do.
>
> There is absolutely *no* reason anyone should ever be ill. Your own personal choices, awareness, and dedication to your health can allow you to stay well. You can be almost immune from the effects of environmental pollution and other things, which you cannot always control.

Aren't some children born with disease?

> Of course certain children are born ill because of choices of the parents and of past generations. They chose these parents knowing this, but this is a different thing. We will talk of this later.
>
> Here is what all can do to strengthen themselves. Build up the immune system and nothing will disturb it. It is *not* true that once you are out of balance and overly sensitive to odors and foods you must live with it all your life. All of that can be overcome with neutralizing individual's allergic reactions, temporarily eliminating certain foods they have become overly sensi-

tive to, and especially with flushing the system with adequate water. This is a major key. Most incarnate are dehydrated. This dehydration causes the cells to deteriorate and create allergic reactions of all kinds, and minor and major diseases.

Now here are some keys to healing. Doris Rapp *(Dr. Rapp is a pediatric allergist and author)* has the solutions to help restore health to so many children and adults, to detoxify schools, homes and the environment. I would suggest her books, *The Impossible Child, Is This Your Child?*, and *Is This Your Child's World?* to begin to understand how to help heal yourselves and your planet. These are not books just for helping children, but for helping to heal every one of all ages.

I also suggest that everyone ready to experience optimum health and heal their diseases read *Your Body's Many Cries For Water: You are Not Sick, You are Thirsty!* by F. Batmanghelidj, M.D. Begin to hydrate your bodies to put them into balance.

You said you were a book reviewer, God, and this is certainly a better way than wading through hundreds of books, not knowing which are really helpful.

There are some very inspirational and helpful books being written. I can suggest, in many ways, books that will aid. One way is to hold a book and ask me about it. I will tell you if it will be helpful and useful for you. I cannot, however, make you read what I have suggested.

> I directed you to the Tony Robbins work. His books and Personal Power Tapes are helpful to you because his collected works motivate you and others. It is harder for most of you to let me motivate you. It is one and the same actually, because who do you think is *his* greatest motivator?

You, of course.

> Of course, just as I am behind all those that try to do good work. Many health theories about water and diet are not entirely correct. There are some very wise and helpful suggestions mixed in with some incorrect information. Breathing exercises, such as many promote are essential to get the oxygen in the body to energize it. Hardly anyone breathes correctly and the cells of most bodies are oxygen-starved just as the cells of most bodies are water-starved.

Then let me get this straight, God. Asking you before eating or drinking anything, hydrating the body, working with breathing exercises, resting, playing, being creative, will restore health and prevent disease?

> Yes, the key is balance, and all these things are keys to that balance. They are laws or guidelines, which enable those in earthly bodies to have optimum health and harmony. Everyone also needs to feel they are doing something to help make a difference in the world, and to make the world a better place. There is an inner knowing of what you came in to do and how to accomplish that. There is a knowing of the many gifts you have come in with. Most who are incarnate just don't let themselves consciously remember.

> There are a few things that you can do to reduce infections and illness almost immediately, until your immune system becomes stronger. You will need to do them consistently. It will create such healthy habits for most of you that you may want to continue them all your life. Wash your hands frequently and keep your hands out of your mouth. Blow your nose more often. Shower daily. Remove your shoes before entering your home and request that others do the same. Take time to be out of doors daily for no less than a half-hour whenever possible. Do not become sleep deprived. You fool yourselves when you think you can be as productive on just a few hours of sleep a night. It weakens your immune system. Almost everyone needs six to twelve hours sleep a night. This is not wasted time.

Blowing your nose more often? That made me laugh. Doing those things will really keep you well?

> In far better health that most currently are.

God, I got off track yesterday afternoon and this morning and wasted so much time. Would you help me understand why? What can I do to stay on track?

> Let up on yourself a little. Yes, you got off track with what you desired to do; but you also got a lot of good things done yesterday. You fed your family well, you allowed two children to have an afternoon of unbridled

joy and play. You read something enjoyable that helps you understand more about women. You were loving and caring with everyone. You listened to me awhile, and you were basically at peace. So it wasn't a wasted day at all. I do not consider it wasted even if you do.

Right now is where the power is. What can you do now, right now, to go in the direction you desire? You can listen to me and let me talk with you. You can do whatever it takes when you reach a standstill: go outside and breathe deeply, lie down and rest, do something entirely different, drink a glass of water, pray, read something uplifting, stretch, whatever helps you change pace and gets you jump-started again. Take time to do long-term planning and short term planning. Make a plan and work that plan, but stay flexible, and above all have some fun doing it. Spend no regret in rehashing things that don't go as you planned. See what you can learn from the experiences and either be easy on yourself or make needed corrections when possible.

Good morning, God.

Good morning Anne. I'm glad you had a happy earth birthday. Lets talk about birthdays. A birthday is a day to celebrate being on the earth, not to measure your life by years nor to buy into the earth consciousness of aging. It would be good if each person would celebrate the anniversary of their arrival into a physical body and acknowledge that they are incarnate and what a gift their life is.

However birthdays have become benchmarks of aging. You allow them to change your consciousness from one of hope to one of depression. You begin to feel life is coming to an end. Therefore the very fact of birthdays and their celebration has become that which adds to the incorrect group consciousness on the planet and shortens life. It does not have to be so. Birthdays are to be celebrated by giving thanks and acknowledging that, as earth time is measured, it is the anniversary of your glorious entrance into the earth plane. Birthdays are to remind you of your divine mission. This would be eminently more helpful than to use birthdays to mark the aging and dying process as is now done.

It's difficult not to think about aging and dying and to be happy about getting older.

When I told you to see how old you would feel if you didn't know how old you were in earth years, and if you didn't have a mirror, you discovered what I wish for all. You discovered that something amazing happens psychologically and physiologically. You ceased to be defined by age. You chose 35 as the age you would be and affirmed it the whole last year. You felt so much better. For 35 in your consciousness, as is true in the conscious minds of most, is the prime of life. That isn't true, as you know. I am going to try to help you understand that 35 means nothing - 85 means nothing - 95 means nothing age-wise - it is simply a mark of your time of entrance in the earth plane. It becomes only what you associate with that age. Because the vast majority of you associate 35 with being in the prime of life and 95 with being elderly, senile and near death, that incorrect knowledge imprints into your whole being. You literally kill yourselves with your thinking earlier than you need to while experiencing this earthly life.

How long should we live or can we live?

120 years on earth should be considered a short period of time. Your bodies are not, like cars, created to become obsolete. In fact you were created to last an indefinite length of time according to how you treat your human vehicle. The earthly laws, if followed, allow the body to continue for hundreds of years to accomplish much good. There are actually dozens of people alive that are 200, 300, 400 and more years old. They live in remote places and are known by those who live there, and a few others. Some of them are called the god men of India and South America, some the women of Africa, some the old ones of Russia and Tibet. Except for a rare few, there are none that live that long in the United States.

Some of the reasons for that are the pollution, the eating habits, and the group consciousness, which is far more destructive in some countries than others. The mental dwelling on aging in America shortens life. In some countries age is treasured and respected, in many it is not.

I want to tell you something else about aging. It is about what thoughts do to the human vehicle. It is not just thoughts regarding aging that cause such destruction and shorten the life expectancy, but thoughts of all kinds that harm emotionally, physically and spiritually.

Yes, I heard years ago that thoughts are things.

To say that thoughts are things is to stop a sentence before completing it. Thoughts are things of power. Thoughts build or destroy, erode or strengthen, always. They flow through you like arrows or feathers, and are directed out through you to others the same. Because birthdays have become benchmarks of aging, humankind's life span has been shortened. If you abide by the earthly laws governing the human form, life would be extended greatly and be in length as it was in times of old. These laws all of you know but have mostly forgotten. You were born knowing and remembering.

When I told you it was not a game to choose what age you would be if you did not know how old you were, you allowed yourself to feel all the earthly vibrations and thought forms of what 35 should be. Then when introduced to the idea of experiencing being 29, you felt the psychological and physiological differences of those thought forms. Now you know what I am trying to re-awaken in all of you. This is not denial of age but embracing power and energy through thought, that ultimately can rejuvenate.

Yesterday, you were given candles on your cake that said 29 years old. You considered letting yourself celebrate what it would feel like to be 29 this coming year. You felt the surge of energy of a 29-year-old and the psychological lift of what you perceive that age to be. So here is my suggestion. Live this next year in the way you think a 29 year old feels, just as you did when claiming what you perceived it like to be 35 years old. Ask yourself what you would do, how you would think, what your energy would be like at that age. Act as if you are 29 for this year. Next year you may chose to experience what 25, 19 or 31 is like. You will experience each differently based on your own preconceptions.

This sounds like denial of how old you really are.

This is not denial of your earthly years, but denial of what you have come to associate with age. It is embracing the vitality of what your mind perceives as younger and more vital. For what you think you become. Mind is truly the builder or destroyer. Every time you say your age say 29, act 29, affirm that you are 29 and you will be amazed at what you will discover. You will feel more energetic. You will begin to look younger. You will begin to see more fully how changing the consciousness of birthday celebrations will change yourself and any that are willing to experiment in such a way. Tell all who will listen about this "experiment" if you will. Tell them I said to try it.

This sounds like a little anti-aging secret, God. It sounds strange and funny but I can't believe the energy and feelings it evokes when I practice it as you have instructed.

I want you to share all the "secrets" I give to you because they are not secrets at all but truths that have gotten swept under the carpet over the centuries and mostly forgotten. I also want you to personally try the things I suggest to you and see for yourself whether or not they work.

Now, knowing and beginning to remember these things, begin in a playful way to become whatever age you choose and hold that consciousness until it no longer suits you, then move on to a different way of feeling.

What about people that are very old and ill and on heavy medication?

Nursing homes are filled with people who have bought into the idea of aging and society's thinking about it. I say to you and to all that will listen, every age is an ideal age. You should choose to work and be productive until you die, or until you shed the form to advance to another level. Nursing homes are also filled with those who didn't understand about their own responsibility of staying healthy and what that entails. They have most often turned to traditional medicine and filled themselves with chemicals from medications of all kinds, which often harms more than helps them. Of course there is a place for medicine and surgery, but it should be the *last* option, not the first, and only after everything else is tried.

Almost all who suffer in such homes are in agony their last years. They suffer from dehydration, over-medication, poor eating habits, and the feeling that they are no longer productive. Now this isn't as over-simplified as you may think.

Chapter 5

Each individual, each person born, is responsible for himself or herself. Most of you turn that responsibility over to doctors and others "experts," schools, and everyone else, when you need to take personal responsibility

There is no aging when you draw strength and vitality from me. There is no wasted time when you are in accord with the divine earthly laws. There is no lack of energy when I am the source.

Your young are old in spirit and your elders die at a time when their wisdom could be of invaluable aid in the healing and transformation of your planet. I did not create it so.

I created you to live disease-free, to live truly long and productive lives; to do work that brings you joy and is of help to others. Yet you live and die again and again and fail to learn these lessons and accept my gifts.

So I have given you this game to play to help you change. Get it right this time - the game of ageless life and power. Become the age you feel, as I have shown you, and count not birthdays as steps on a ladder to death, but steps on a golden stairway to abundant life.

Be the age you associate with power and youth. This association will serve until you learn to play the game of life and remember the guidelines by which to live. Then you will die fully aware and not from disease or your own incorrect thoughts. You will release from your present form when you have completed your task, then and only then. Even for those in nursing homes and in ill health, this game can make the remaining years so much better and happier.

You must change the thoughts and associations you have to each year of life if you are to live long, healthy and productive lives. You must act as if you are always young and full of vitality; and so you will be.

What about those who are dying or about to die?

For some, it is time to transition and release the weakened and worn physical shell, and let the soul float free.

Those of you who believe in what I am reminding you of must set the example. There will be those who laugh and say this is denial of aging. You yourself have so questioned. But it is not; it is the embracing of the life force available to all of you as you get in accord with the natural laws governing your life form and this planet. Great untapped power is available to accomplish anything and everything your soul calls you to do, for as long as it takes to do it.

MESSAGES FROM GOD

CHAPTER 6

…God on… Jesus, Mary, the Bible,
prayer, religion…and the devil…

God, I recently heard a minister on television say that his congregation had things too easy. He said he wished they would have bad things happen to them and start suffering, so they would have to turn to you for help.

> That is foolishness, Anne. You don't believe that for a minute.

No, I don't.

> But thousands do believe this way. That is not how I am. I don't ever want you to suffer. I want you make each day one of joy. I want you to make a paradise of earth and delight in it. I want you to find ways to end your suffering, not make it worse. I do not test you. I

do not punish you. If you are suffering you have either created it or allowed it to happen. That is always true. I am your creator and your friend. Would a friend delight in seeing a friend suffer? A resounding *NO*.

I believe that, God.

I know you do, Anne. I just wanted to set the record straight. I wish you didn't punish yourselves and suffer. It never has been or ever will be my way. As long as authority figures tell people incorrect things about how I am, and they believe them, they will suffer. That's why everyone needs to listen to me him or herself.

How can we know and understand you better and not get misled?

The pathway in life is straight and narrow. It goes directly from you to me. You come into this life with a roadmap back to me engraved on your soul. You forget you have this roadmap and struggle the whole lifetime to find your direction. There are signs all along the way; but you ignore most of them. You swerve from right to left, back up, turn around, get mired in the mud, pull over and park, then race wildly ahead to make up for lost time, and crash into someone else stopped on the road. You patch up your vehicle, take off again, ask someone for directions, then follow them awhile. Soon you swerve off on a side road realizing that you've been directed incorrectly. After being lost for some time and suffering various difficulties, you slowly return to the road and cautiously proceed. This time you are sure you know how to get where you're going. You even recognize some of the highway signs and find them on the map you didn't realize you had in your pocket. You finally have the right directions, and off you go at last. Then your vehicle breaks down completely; and, you still haven't reached your destination. An entire lifetime can be wasted this way.

You turn to others for answers instead of to me. You follow their thinking rather than your own thinking directed by me.

Why would any leaders try to instill such fear of you and your wrath?

It is a form of control. It shows a clear lack of listening to me. Some of it is done because of their own fears, taught to them in their early years by those who also feared. Some teach such erroneous things about me because they believe I will actually punish people that don't follow these guilt-producing rules. They feel unless they put "the fear of God" into everyone that they will suffer eternal hell and damnation. Deep inside they know this isn't my way; but for so long they have suppressed my leadings that they become more and more hardened to my loving guidance.

How many souls have suffered because of those who tell others the great lies about me. I am not a vengeful God. I am not a jealous God. I am not a condemning God. I am not a God of wrath. I love my creation and none of them can ever do anything to keep me from loving them. I would not punish them. They will create their own self-punishment for the things they feel they have done incorrectly. They will make of life a hell, not the heaven it is. They will never let themselves remember that the heaven on earth is within them.

As a child I heard "fire and brimstone" sermons often. It was scary sometimes. I would tell my mother that the minister said God was going to punish me if I did something wrong. She would always tell me that she knew that was what ministers said, and even the Bible had such things in it. She assured me that she didn't think God was like that and that he loved me and wouldn't punish me. We eventually stopped going to either my father's or my mother's church.

> Good for your mother. That's the reason it's been easier for us to talk. You have never been afraid of me; and, you learned to believe what your mother told you first, then to trust what you felt in your heart about me.
>
> Can you imagine what many children feel about me? You would not believe what so many of them are taught. Can you imagine the spiritual and emotional scars so many adults have because of what they were taught to believe about me? One day they will all know the truth; but entire incarnations are limited by the guilt, fears and mind control of such teachings.

Is there a particular religion that is nearer to teaching the truth about you?

> No. Many contain *some* truths about me and the empowering spiritual laws governing the earth. Many contain no helpful truths that enable their followers to make joyful spiritual growth. Some teach untruths that cause many to stumble and delay their growth for a lifetime.

For instance, the Mormons have the *Book of Mormon,* translated with my help by Joseph Smith. It is an accurate historical account of the early inhabitants who came across the ocean from other lands to the North and South American continents. It could be studied by all for greater historical and spiritual understanding. Joseph Smith remembered and often listened to me.

There are many wonderful programs for youth and adults within that particular religion. However, there are many things that are taught that are not my teachings and were the erroneous thinking of those who did not listen to me. Baptism for the dead, celestial marriage and the wearing of garments are some.

Since I do not judge polygamy, other than it is not ideal in today's world; it is of little consequence spiritually what I am going to share with you. If the old records and newspaper accounts were checked accurately from the time of Joseph Smith you would discover that he was against polygamy. He spoke against it, never taught such, and Emma Smith was his one and only wife, as she so testified and recorded on her deathbed. This basic teaching attributed to him shows how historical information is perpetuated incorrectly for generations because of another person's teaching. Then others take this untruth and add to it. This incorrect teaching has caused many to refuse to look at the many truths in this religion that could actually be helpful.

The Catholics have much ceremony that is spirit lifting. Confession can be a therapeutic and healing experience. The blessing of babies and their dedication is a spiritual step in the right direction. Many fine souls are drawn to this religion with the right intent.

To have a doctrine that requires celibacy of the leaders who may or may not chose such, is not my will. Teaching that all but one kind of birth control is a sin, is not my spiritual teaching. All the guilt put on children and adults regarding sexuality is an attempt to make something ugly out of something beautiful I created. Much harm and delay of soul growth has come because of these and other teachings that can never bring peace to my creation.

There is much good to be said for the Jewish faith. It is a worthwhile attempt to keep tradition going, which many find spiritually uplifting. There are sacred days celebrated that enable the followers to pause, reflect and be thankful. There is a clannish link that makes most feel part of a huge family with roots from the past and hope for the future. Many are especially nurturing with their children. In Jewish mysticism there is much truth taught about a greater awareness. Yet there is a void that many feel because it becomes difficult for them to allow other truth to be considered without releasing the old teachings that no longer apply or serve them.

Much good has been done in the name of those who are Christians; but, much harm has also been done. This is such a broad grouping going from fundamentalism and out in a thousand directions. Any religion that teaches I am a vengeful God and that you will go to hell if you don't follow my rules, is not in accord with me. Any religion that teaches they are the *only* right religion is sadly fooling themselves. Any religion teaching that every word in the Bible is true is simply not listening to me. I haven't finished speaking and some of my words have been garbled. A religion that teaches I am a God of love and practices the Great Commandment is headed in the right direction.

And on it goes, Anne. We could discuss the pros and cons of each religion, the strengths and weaknesses, but you get the idea.

Yes, but don't the so-called new age religions seem to have more of the truths that you are sharing here?

Again, yes and no. Some teach that I still speak today, but no one actually listens. Many get so involved with what they call paranormal phenomenon as being the spiritual sign of what is true, that they lose sight of other spiritual gifts and teachings. You can feel the lack of real spirit in their activities. Others lack trained leaders to keep them cohesive and in tune with my spirit. Some have helpful and hopeful teachings, but go financially unsupported by their participants and eventually cease to be able to provide their spiritual ministry. Many groups with great spiritual potential that try to teach my truths have such a mixture of individuals from so many other religions and teachings that no group could satisfy such diverse expectations. They soon close their doors, too.

My hand is on every religious organization, every teaching, each leader, each participant. Some follow my leadings, most don't. There is no one teaching that gets more of my spirit. They are all equal. It is just that some individuals listen to my guidance and many don't. I am a God of "thou-shalts" not of "thou-shalt-nots."

It can be helpful to meet and participate in a spiritual group working on oneness together. There can be great power raised in such a gathering. If you find such a group, attend, support and participate with them. Pray and work together for the good of each other and humankind. Find not fault with individuals and unimportant things; but experience my presence among you.

If you are not inclined to be part of a group, make time daily to read something that lifts your spirit. Pray for others and yourself and talk with me. Listen and trust my guidance. Spend time expanding your spiritual awareness.

That's helpful, God. I understand this more.

I have a talk to prepare on "Our Rocky Relationship with the Bible." Can you help me with what to say to encourage others to read and understand this misunderstood book?

Equate the Bible to a relationship. There are strengths and difficulties in every relationship; yet, as you build on the strengths and understand the difficulties, the relationship grows and becomes better and better from the understanding. Hopefully, you don't throw away the relationship because it has some imperfections. You build on the things that are good, and overlook some of the warts.

Pick some of the most beautiful scriptures, and some of the ones that people stumble on. Then, speak from your own experiences and from your heart. Tell them not to let others' interpretations of the Bible take the gems of truth from them by claiming all authority and ownership of what was written. Also, tell them to read it with an understanding that the confusing statements are what men *thought* I was like. Even so, just as you can see how incorrect parts of it are, much of what you still believe to be correct is incorrect. So, it's a good learning tool.

Tell them how you ask me to show you what I really mean when you read the Bible. That's a good way to approach it. Tell them they need their own Bible, that is exclusively theirs, so they can mark it up and underline it and put question marks in it and ask me about it. It's worth studying. Despite its faults and inaccuracies, it has been a best seller for a long time. If you're willing to work with it and harvest the gems of truth it contains without throwing it all away because it is obviously mistranslated and erroneous in parts, then you will find much help from it.

It has been a best seller. You're right. You mean you want me to write what I do each time I read a version of the *Bible*, whether the King James Version, *The Living Bible* or George Lamsa's translation of the *Bible from the Aramaic of the Peshitta* text?

Yes, Anne.

I always begin with this prayer: "God as I read this, show me the truth and what you truly mean, that I may grow in understanding. Help your words of truth heal and bless me in every way that I may fulfill my soul purpose as you have created me to do."

> That's good. It works for you, doesn't it? People can put their request in their own words; and, I can help make this book more meaningful in their life.

Yes, each time I seem to sense what is true and what isn't, as I read the verses. I also have an understanding of certain passages that I never did before.

> That's the way you'll learn best from anything you read; and, that's the way to encourage people to read the Bible.

There is so much confusion about the man called Jesus and about him being your "only begotten son." Some Bible historians interpret "only begotten" as *special*, not *only*. Would you explain more about him?

> Jesus was my *special* son. He was not my *only* son. Every soul incarnate is my special son or daughter. I was as joyful about each of you entering the earth experience as I was about him entering. Just as you are proud of a child who works hard and accomplishes much, that is what this soul did. He became all a parent could have hoped for and more. What he came to show was that you too can do anything you choose to accomplish. Not by you doing all he did but by

doing other things that your soul calls you to do. You might choose to accomplish your soul mission by painting the most beautiful paintings, helping children in need, writing helpful and life-changing books, making inspirational movies. You can accomplish great works by having a pure heart and unconditional love for yourself and others. You can fulfill your soul purpose by doing the most mundane chores and jobs with an attitude of joy and love and by asking my help and direction. This is the Christ-way; it is open to any who choose it.

What you do is unimportant - unless you choose to do something that keeps you from accomplishing the soul mission you set for yourself before entering. The solitary mission for your soul growth might be one small act of kindness. It might be choosing to be an attorney for the poor or being active in politics to try and make a difference. *How* you accomplish what you set for yourself is the key. How - the attitude, the love, the sincerity, the caring with which you do it. Then you may graduate on to other things. Some of you may have dozens of goals you have set for your soul to accomplish. Again, do them the very best with all your body, mind and spirit, with your heart and soul, step-by-step. Does not the person scrubbing the floors, who prays as they work, who loves others, who is working in such a way to help someone else, do a greater spiritual work than the millionaire businessman who takes shortcuts and hurts and exploits others? Of course. Everyone's soul mission is a great mission. Is not one true kindness in a lifetime as great as ruling a country or being president of a company? I say it is.

No job anyone does is greater than the job another does. I see all work as equal. I see and love all souls exactly the same. There is no black, no white, any male or female, any gay or straight, any fat or thin, any ugly or beautiful, any poor or rich, any failures or successes, no ghetto or society soul. You would do well to see it the same.

The man Jesus, who became Christed because of his choices and his love, is simply an example for all. It has been said that Jesus measured up to the law of love and made each choice with which he was faced in accord with that law. That is correct. Others have become Christs because of their choices throughout many times and in many places. You each have such potential.

This truth will also not be popular among those who have been incorrectly taught such, but Jesus was never meant to be worshipped. Believe in him, yes, but that belief should be in his example for you. Many are confused as to whether he is God. He is as much God as you are. For haven't I told you we are one? Yet as much as we are all one, each soul is spirit unto itself also, for I am in you yet around you.

Did Jesus really die for our sins as is often taught?

He died because humankind's thoughts and errors created the hostile world; yet, he lived and died to show you the way. He allowed himself to be killed. He did rise from the dead, to be the pattern and wayshower for all, no matter what race or religion. His life and his death were gifts he gave to future generations, too. His stories, his promises, his example were his legacy.

He could not die for anyone's sins. There are no sins. There is simply falling short of being your best and there are delays and detours from exercising your free will and choices. When you fall short, try again and again until you do whatever it is the way that would serve you and others best. Jesus chose to measure up to the best within himself, always. Everyone incarnate has this potential. Jesus lived and died to show you the way home to me and to show you about yourselves and how to live while you have an earthly body. He is the most loving pattern for the planet earth.

Was Jesus born of a virgin? Is that story true?

Remember that I told you that there was no male involved in his birth; but his birth was not so different from yours. An egg and a sperm do not of themselves create life. It is always and only my touch, my energy that enters and ignites the linking of sperm and egg, which creates the conception. So, there is no conception without my touch. In the conception of both Jesus and his Mother, Mary, no male was involved, only my touch.

You are his brothers and sisters; he is your Elder Brother. Believe that if you use him as an example, a pattern to be like, that you too may one day be a Christ to another universe.

You mean we could be a Jesus to another place?

Not a Jesus, for, again, Jesus is the man who became a Christ. But, yes, you can grow to become a Christ elsewhere, and do even greater works than he did.

I could never do that.

No, not right now. Greater works just means different works but just as great in their own way. You could learn to be so filled with love that you and everyone else could evolve to that.

I don't want to.

You don't have to, but one day you probably will.

I can barely handle this life, and I don't live it that spiritually sometimes.

Yes, but when you learn to handle it, you will have taken another step toward that promise.

I need to process this awhile. This is something to think about.

Then we will talk when you are ready. Anne, when people hear what they're not used to or that which conflicts with their previous beliefs and programming, they want to stop listening. So, I'll help you through some of this. This would have been blasphemy in the church you grew up in, wouldn't it? Actually, I tried to tell you and many others these same things even then. You did not hear me clearly. Truth is never blasphemy.

OK, I'm ready to hear some more about all this.

> Here is what happened. As I told you that there is no conception without my touch. A sperm and egg coming together cannot create life. I am actively involved in each conception, even when it may not be ideal, but is of the choosing of two people. There are no accidental conceptions. Many are not ideal and cause great pain, but none are accidental.

What do you mean? A child born from a rape, teenagers experimenting with sex who conceive, menopausal women getting pregnant - these pregnancies are not accidental? What about people who try hard to conceive and can't get pregnant?

> None of these is an accident as you would perceive it, nor is it unplanned and without acceptance by both parties. When a mature and caring couple marry, come together to create a life together, make a commitment to each other and to the rearing of a child, it is ideal. Ideal in that the child has a greater chance of reaching a higher level of spiritual growth than if there is no such love and preparation. Ideal in that they will be raised by a father and mother and receive the best of both of their awareness.
>
> Suppose two teenagers fall in love in high school, truly care about each other, continue with their caring through college and decide to marry. They talk about the kind of home life they want, and plan and prepare

for a family. Souls waiting to enter whatever vehicles are available will find this an easier and more loving situation into which to incarnate. You might call these two examples easier incarnations for the most part. The child enters, grandly welcomed by the parents and extended family, and has a most auspicious start. Throughout their life there is a strong foundation of faith, love and a desire to work and help others. They may or may not do a good life's work, according to their choices, the lessons they came to learn, and a variety of other influences; but the odds are they will have a balanced and productive life.

Now take a young woman raised in poverty, unable to finish high school because of difficulties in the home, lack of enough income even to cover basic necessities and lack of proper parenting and love. She as a teenager meets a young man from similar circumstances and they fall in love or have sexual relations. Because neither has been properly nurtured since childhood, they have no strong foundation upon which to build a family life. Both need many things they have lacked when growing up and try to find that in each other. A pregnancy occurs.

Souls, in the dimension you call the sprit plane, waiting to enter a body, discuss the odds of being able to accomplish what they need to by entering with these two parents. They know it will not be an easy incarnation, being born to young and immature parents, who have themselves been improperly raised to think of anything much greater than survival. Certain of these souls realize they could come in and be of help in the situation. Other souls realize that difficult lessons they need to learn could possibly be learned through this less than ideal sojourn. Some souls choose not to enter these difficult unions, or several souls may want the chance of entering this situation. They have many meeting with helpers who advise them. They also meet with the expectant parents and sometimes their families, when they sleep and are out of their physical bodies, and discuss the strengths and weakness of the associations.

Many decisions are made in both dimensions. Sometimes days and months pass before a soul is selected and chooses to enter and the parents also agree to allow that soul to enter. Almost always there has been some previous connection between these souls before, or there would not be the attraction to coming together to work things out and to make spiritual growth.

For the parents and families that prepare and are themselves more aware and mature, it is a great experience for the soul and for themselves. Under the more difficult circumstances, the soul enters with powerful and good intentions of helping the parents and extended family, but then gets caught up as years go by in the day to day struggle of life. Forgetting its origin and commitment when awake, the soul is in a constant struggle most of that incarnation and often is faced with even more difficult lessons than the parents.

Almost every night all the souls involved, when asleep and out of their physical bodies, meet together with helpers and angels and discuss things to do and ways to improve their situations. For those who have prepared themselves better, the lessons they learn in these sessions help them in the decisions they make for their families many times. When those who have not prepared themselves as well wake up they may have some insights that would help, but they either disregard these feelings or are so caught up in survival that they forget. Year after year helpers work with them, often to no avail.

Preparation before marriage, before contemplating a pregnancy, and before the birth of a child simply creates possibilities of greater soul growth. Are there exceptions? Of course. There are many exceptions; but even those exceptions find the pathway to their goal more difficult many of the times.

Mary, the one who was chosen to be the mother of the soul that would become Jesus, prepared for years for the possibility of this birth. She and many young women in the Essene community at that time gladly and lovingly went through many years of instructions and disciplines. That Joseph who married her and helped in raising Jesus was shocked and wanted to hide her pregnancy is simply untrue. All of those in the community worked together in allowing this soul to enter.

There is some information in the Edgar Cayce readings about Mary and the birth of Jesus that is similar to this. Is that information basically correct and would it be helpful to read it?

Yes, it would. I spoke often to Edgar Cayce who now helps many from another dimension, as you know. He and I had and still have deeply philosophical discussions; and, he heard me correctly much of the time.

Could you talk a little more about Mary? I have never been taught to worship her, but I have always admired her and what she went through.

> She is not meant to be worshipped. Let me first tell you what it was like when all thought of God as Mother. Of course I am neither, but imagine the feeling women had when they perceived me as Mother. It gave women a deep personal feeling of self worth because the creator was a woman like them.
>
> Mary is to be a pattern for women. Like Jesus is a pattern, a wayshower, Mary too is such a pattern, but especially for women. Mary's life, her commitment, all that she did, was to be as a light on the pathway, and to show the way for others. Her preparation for pregnancy is one that would benefit all to understand. For, you see, it began long before she was born. Mary's mother's mother, her grandmother, was a great woman with deep spiritual understanding. She was a woman of her time who was not like the ordinary. She was a part of the Essene group but not living in the community.
>
> Her parents and family were practitioners of the faith; but they were unable to physically live in the community. She met whenever possible with others of like mind. So, the preparation began there. She prepared herself to give birth to Mary's mother, making all those preparations that Mary herself would make many years later. It takes several generations for preparation for certain souls - let's call them spiritual avatars - to enter. Mary was such. Jesus was such. There were many others.

Then, being raised with love, caring and deep awareness herself, Mary's mother prepared for Mary's birth. There was no male involved in Mary's conception either, only my touch. That was because of the faith and purpose of Mary's mother, and to begin to show the world at that time how my spirit can touch earth in a variety of ways. Much of this information has been lost, or is not easily found; but it can be located with some perseverance.

From the moment Mary was conceived, her mother knew she was carrying a most special soul for an important work to be done. She knew that the avatar of the age was to come through her daughter. She knew she was to have a daughter, for I told her so. There needed to be a purity for her entrance - a purity of genetics - to create souls of this magnitude. Yet, let me emphasize, never did I intend for Mary to be worshipped as some religions now do, and did even then. She was not to be worshipped but her choices and patterns were to be emulated. She was to be seen as a pattern for womankind in this age and the vehicle for the avatar Jesus. Each age has been given this gift of an avatar. This is the first age that has so adulterated the teachings. This is not the first age that killed the avatar or messenger.

The soul, the avatar Jesus, was not to be worshipped. When he said what he did others could do and greater works than these, he truly meant that. And, when he said "believe in me," it was not worship me, but believe in me so you will believe in yourself. He confirmed that you are gods, children of the most high - most high meaning *me*.

I understand this better now.

> Much of what you know and have learned and now believe is true, Anne; but you are in the minority on this earth. The few of you who believe must teach the masses who do not yet remember. Re-awaken them to me and to who they really are. From the beginning of time I have always worked through certain individuals who are searching for truth and whose own consciousness can be moved aside to hear me speak. Edgar Cayce is one such example. Yogananda, Buddha and Sai Baba are others, as are many in the Bible and sacred texts. It is possible to speak through those who speak in many different languages. Many I speak to consent to bring through information, which is foreign to what they have been taught or believe, in order to bring truth to the world.
>
> So don't let learned others, or those with some but not the fullness of truth, mislead or cause you to doubt. Listen to *me*, to your higher self, to ourselves and let me direct you. This is what Mary did, what her mother and grandmother did, and what her son did.

Is there a devil or satan?

> There is evil and there is negativity. Everything is energy. Positive and negative energy finds like energy and attaches to it until there is a big ball of energy that is almost an entity in itself. There are ways to dissolve

the destructive energy that you think of as evil. First, acknowledge it and don't pretend it isn't there. Secondly, know that you are always stronger than it is; and you can change and redirect it. If you doubt that you can do this, have other people join you in prayer; and, you can break up the negative energy and dissolve it into another form. The energy always continues; but it can continue in various forms. Your thoughts and actions can mold it into a positive form. Thirdly, you can send such good energy, through thought, prayer, and affirmations, to this negative energy that in dissolving it to a form of more positive energy, it then has power to go about its business of helping, not hurting. I do not judge the energy, for one day it will all be transformed to a positive vibration. You need always keep aware that you do not let yourself get engulfed in energy that does not strengthen but weakens.

There are solitary individuals or souls that *unconsciously* disrupt, both among the living and the dead. There are individual and small groups of souls that joy in disruption, among both the living and the dead, because of their lack of spiritual awareness. Many of them become energy drainers. I would have you call these what they are, disruptive forces. That many incarnate do not want to acknowledge such does not make these energies any less disruptive or draining.

How do you protect yourself from such?

By keeping your vibrations strong and high so they cannot impact on you. Here's how this is done: Everything that you eat, think, do, and imagine is a vibration and is absorbed by the energy sac that is you. It can change, disrupt and influence your vibration in a very negative way; or, it can influence in a positive way. A person can immediately change in an instant or carry a vibration for many years, or lifetimes. The more in harmony or positive your vibration, the less any out of harmony or disruptive vibration can affect you.

Your dreams warn you when some one or ones are trying to harm you. *You* know this by the dreams you have had of Dobermans, doors open and people trying to shoot you. You remembered these dreams because a person and a group of persons were actually trying to harm you. You can use these dreams as a call to prayer. Immediately pray for help from those in the spirit plane assigned to you: angels, masters, Jesus, me. It works. You acknowledge your own weakness, call for stronger help and it immediately comes. That permanently discourages those trying to do you harm physically, emotionally, spiritually. It gives you a breather as you check to see what changes you need to make to protect yourself more fully from further disruption and keep the wolves at bay. If you don't make mental, spiritual or physical changes to shield yourself from their negative vibrations, then the wolves return again and again. Instead of being able to get about your work, you may either get drained, depressed and discouraged, which they love for you to do. Always remember that your light is stronger than any darkness and negativity. When you feel unable to withstand the negativity sent to you, ask that angels stand between you and those who would disrupt.

– ✡ –

You said we would talk more about the Ten Commandments?

> The commandments, though somewhat erroneous through misinterpretation and changes, were never meant to scold or create guilt. They were meant to empower. For each, when properly understood, helps you be in accord with the natural laws of your dimension. They are not limiting but strengthening. Let me help you better understand these commandments, which are better called guidelines or suggestions. For instance, "Thou shalt not kill." Sometimes one kills to save another. Sometimes one accepts being killed to save another. Other times one accepts being killed to save many others. Exceptions to these guidelines do not lessen their value to help you have a better, more balanced and peaceful life when correctly understood. An incarnation experience is a sacred gift for a soul and should be treasured. Life is precious and to take another's life, is a serious act. What you do that is out of accord with the highest truth within you, will one day have to be met. You will meet the lesson in this or another lifetime, to work it out in a better way. To take the life of another person is something that causes all kinds of energies to come into play.

Wouldn't killing someone to save your life or the life of a loved one be acceptable, if a person were trying to kill you or them?

> This would be decided by the soul on an individual basis. For some it would be an acceptable thing to do, for some it would not.

Chapter 6

What about capital punishment?

> This would best be understood by a true awareness about the return of souls in other bodies and life after death. Sometimes souls have so allowed themselves to be consumed by negativity that they murder and commit atrocious crimes against others. They need to be prevented from such actions. Some few can get healed and turn their lives around while incarcerated, even though they will never be allowed to rejoin society.
>
> Others will not respond to any type of treatment while incarnate. In those cases a more humane way would be to release the individual from the physical body and give them a chance to learn and grow in the spirit realm. They can often make more progress in healing their negativity and obsessions in that realm. If they choose not to progress, they will continue to be worked with for as long as it takes until they do. They will not be allowed to return in another body until their helpers feel they have made sufficient growth to meet their lessons on earth in a better way than before.
>
> So you see, there is no one answer to either of your questions. Each situation needs evaluation in a variety of ways. There are currently in prisons some who would benefit from the death penalty but who are kept imprisoned for decades without any soul progress being made. Others are put to death when there were ways in which they could have made much progress in their soul development even in prison. Until there is more understanding and sensitivity regarding this issue, it will not be resolved in the best spiritual way.

We have discussed the adultery commandment; but, let's do one more. Then at another time we will talk about the rest of them. "Thou shalt have no other gods before me." Anything that takes your attention and focus away from your relationship with me is a false god. Everything that comes between you and fulfilling your soul mission is a false god. I never said I was a jealous God; but men added that and left out much, according to their own biases and fears. They often were willing to experience my supposed wrath, to eliminate things from the teachings that they thought would take away something they and others enjoyed doing.

All addictions are false gods, but some false gods creep in so subtly that you hardly see them for what they are. A few examples are over-attention to the physical body and looks, the need to be a messiah to everyone, television, computers, shopping and over-attention to order. As you think upon it, you may discover your own false gods.

Why does it seem so many prayers are not answered?

As you choose it, so it will be. Claim, don't *ask* or *want*, and it will be. *Choose* rather than *want*. *Declare* a thing. Then it will be done. *Be thankful in advance*, knowing that what you have prayed will be. It will be. Then continue in a state of thanksgiving and expectation in all things that you declare.

> In *choosing*, I can help you. In *wanting* I cannot so easily. *Choosing* brings to you what you desire. *Wanting* puts up a barrier.
>
> Everything is energy and thought. *Claim, declare* and *choose* are powerful words. *Asking, wanting* are weakening both to you and to the universe. You have asked in the name of Jesus all your life. Now "declare, claim and choose" in Jesus' name, in *my* name, and in your name, too, and you empower yourself.
>
> *Tried* is the wrong word; it disempowers you. Try suggests you may fail, try suggests pain and effort. Give thanks in advance for all you choose.
>
> Now here is something else I want to tell you. The fact that you want to listen to me and are determined to get my guidance out to others whatever that takes, is exactly what I had prayed for.

You pray God? To whom?

> To myself and to all of my creation. I pray it in all our names. When I pray, believe me, that energy is felt throughout the universes.

I bet it is. I pray too God, how far do my prayers go?

> Some of your prayers make it to the next room, some to the people being prayed for, some to the angels, some across the oceans. It depends upon your purpose, sincerity, and the power you allow to flow and enrich your heart at the time. But always I hear, and your prayers always reach me.

I like that. They always reach you. Then I'm in good hands.

> Your prayers and thoughts put you in spiritual and telepathic rapport with the person you are praying for or thinking about. When you pray for someone whom you know is filled with such pain that they are directing harmful thoughts to you, or wish you ill, forgive them as I have shared. But, in addition, you may ask that I stand between them and you until their pain is healed. This breaks the telepathic link between you until they become more at peace. You can also ask that the Master Jesus or an angel stand between you and direct healing to the person. There are times when your prayers in such a situation are better directed through a stronger power. You will sense when this is needed.

Would you tell me some more about how prayer works?

> I will tell you this again and again, you must trust and believe that your prayers will be answered when you pray. All things are possible and will happen if you but trust and believe. If you would see your prayers answered, you need not plead or beseech me. You need but give thanks that your prayer is answered; and, from that moment on act as if it has already been answered. How would you act when the prayer is answered? This is important to do. However, along with that attitude, be ever aware of the many ways in which your prayer is being answered from the moment it is prayed, and before it is prayed. Watch for the many answers that I send you.

Chapter 6

Is it true that you know what we need before we pray?

> Yes, I know what you need far before you are aware of what you need and desire. Often I have been speaking to you for long periods of time before you feel you need to ask my help. I send thoughts to you of those things which would aid you. I send others to you to bring the help you seek. I speak through all the beauties of nature to raise your spirit to hear me more fully. I speak and lead you in a thousand ways. Yet, because I do not speak the way *you* expect, the way *you* want me to answer, you refuse to hear me. Soon you become discouraged, believing I do not answer. Before long you become angry that I have not answered you. Finally you stop asking or even trying to hear my answers.
>
> I will tell you a great truth. A truth you will not like to hear. But, like all great truths, you must unlearn much of what you have erroneously been taught in order to hear it and to take a next step in growth.
>
> I do not answer prayer. Not in the way you have been taught to believe.

What? That can't be true. Then why have I prayed all these years? I've wasted all that time and thought you heard me and answered my prayers. How come so many of my prayers were answered or seemed to be answered? This is the worst thing you have ever told me.

> *You* answer your prayers. I just send you suggestions to help you get your prayers answered. Let me explain it so you won't feel discouraged but encouraged.

I'm not going to feel encouraged no matter what you say. Because if you're God and you don't answer prayers, then why even believe in you?

> Well, let me try. Do you remember a saying you first liked then threw away: Prayer doesn't change things, prayer changes people and people change things?

Yes, but I found I didn't believe it.

> Believe it. It wasn't wrong. It's true. Prayer isn't understood and people have many misconceptions about prayer. They start thinking that if they pray louder, longer, repeat their pleas over and over, burn enough candles, torture themselves to show me they are sincere, deprive themselves of something they enjoy, cry enough, scream loud enough, bang on the door long enough, that I will have to give them what they are asking for.
>
> When they don't think I have answered despite all their sacrifices, they are not very happy with me, or with their religion or with themselves even. Especially with themselves. Many think they haven't prayed long enough, hard enough. They give extra money, and deprive themselves even more. After awhile they are really distraught and angry at me and at themselves for believing in me. Or, they think they're unworthy and that I don't love them enough to answer.

I have done and felt all those things at times.

> Let me tell you how prayer works and then decide for yourself how you feel. I have to begin this by saying,

you can't *not* believe in me. I am you and you are me. Not believing in me is not believing in yourself and in your holy creation. You can say you don't believe in me, but everyone in their soul believes in me because they know me. On the soul level everyone is conscious that we are all one. Everyone. On the conscious level not everyone lets himself or herself remember. So, knowing this creates the foundation of what I am going to tell you about prayer.

Prayer is directed and undirected thought. Every thought that you have is a prayer. It affects you, everything around you, every person, plant, rock, and animal. Let's for this discussion divide thoughts into two categories: harmonious and strengthening thoughts and inharmonious and weakening thoughts. Directed and undirected thoughts both have these two categories. What you refer to as prayer is most often directed thought. You construct in your mind something you want to ask me for, someone you want healing for, or thanks that you want to express for something. If these are constructed and worded well they become harmonious and strengthening thoughts that emanate from you in all directions. Some specific prayer-thoughts are directed more specifically to certain individuals you are concerned about. Nevertheless they also broadcast from you in many directions as well as to the specific person.

Undirected thought-prayers are sometimes the way you talk to yourself in your mind as you think about people and situations that bother you. These may be harmonious or inharmonious depending on their content. The more undirected thoughts you have the easier it is to get in a habit of broadcasting disharmony outward from you and letting it manifest inside you. So be as watchful of your mind chatter as the words you verbalize.

These thought-prayers, of many kinds, go out like radio waves. They can bombard an individual that you are thinking ill of with much negativity. They can also bombard someone who is sick with much positive energy as you ask for healing for them. This energy bombardment is happening all the time with everyone. You are constantly sending-receiving-sending. Your harmonious prayers and thoughts for an individual who is ill, for instance, are received by them, and become part of the pattern of information they consider and the energy they use to get well, or to release from the physical body. There are dozens, sometimes hundreds, of bits of thought-energy going toward that person from many sources. The energy finds its way almost like a magnet to the one it is meant for. It matters not whether you use a name, see the photograph of a person, or, if unable to remember their name, think about them and their situation. The thought-energy finds them and flows into and around them.

They are also broadcasting their own thoughts and needs and often you will receive this energy, and it causes you to think of them. You then send them a prayer-thought which they receive again, and on it goes.

Sometimes you call on angels, and as that prayer-thought is received, angels go where asked to take that prayer and healing. They, unlike you, know, when they are around the ill person, whether or not the person plans to stay in the physical form or leave. With this knowing, they help as needed. At times the soul is planning to exit the body and the angels know the soul has work yet to do. They encourage the soul to remain; and the angels help in whatever way they can. However, the soul makes that final decision and can override the angel's suggestions. It rarely does, but it can.

The prayers being sent to this person who is ill, help greatly in whatever way is needed, whether in leaving or staying in earthly form. There are times when the prayers of a person or family are so intense that the soul knows it needs to leave the body; but it stays to comfort the family awhile longer. This is something to be aware of. Since most of you see death incorrectly, as an ending, rather than a new beginning or completion of the earthly task, do not pray to hold the soul in the body when it may be time to leave.

Learn to compose your prayer-thoughts in a more powerful and healing way. First, never pray that the person be healed if it is my will. It is always my will that the person be healed. You and I just have different awareness of what healing is. There is physical healing, mental and emotional healing, soul healing, and release healing from the physical form when the earthly sojourn is over. A better prayer-thought, or words to this end, might be, "God direct angels and prayers to this person that they are healed in the way that is best for their soul growth. Show me what I can do to be of the greatest help to this person." So, even though I don't answer your prayers, you need to pray to put yourself in attunement with me and all about you, so that your prayers have the most effect. I will always be at your side, suggesting, coaching and leading you.

This would be very difficult to pray this way for a child who was ill.

Yes, it is particularly hard when you are praying for a child. You forget that the child is only young in earthly years, but is old in soul years. You forget that even if the child dies, you are not separated, but still together on a soul level. You forget that you never lose anyone; and, you will always be together with those you love. You are just held in different palms of my hand; and, you meet in other rooms of the house of the soul, as I have told you.

The more frantic a prayer, the less trust and faith there usually is. Let me explain it this way. You pray for an ill friend or family member. That prayer-thought reaches them and is as a healing balm. You continue praying, trusting and believing your prayers are helpful, and each of these prayers finds its way to the person and flows in and out of their vibrations. Then your prayers get more and more intense and frantic as doubt moves in and you don't yet see the person improving as you want. Those prayers also reach the person but they do not help. They come in as agitated vibrations out of harmony with the vibrations of the person. At times they can even disturb the healing energy field of the person.

Be careful what you pray for, your prayers may be answered. There is a lot of truth in that statement. Think of the things you have prayed for in your life.

> Perhaps a relationship you wanted that you later discovered wasn't the right one for you. A particular job that you pleaded for in your prayers, then found a better one, and met the person of your heart there.
>
> I do not deny these prayers. They go out to the person or situation and that thought is considered by them and with others – sometimes by a few others, sometimes hundreds and thousands. Thoughts go back and forth between you and the person or persons involved, and both of you decide on what is best for each of your souls. Angels may be there to help. Certainly I send help and suggestions to all of you regarding your decision. Sometimes you listen, often you don't. Many times you are very thankful your prayer seemingly was not answered. It was answered. Just in a different way than you prayed.

Then we should not pray and ask you for anything because you aren't going to answer us anyway?

> No, that's not what I said. You should pray and ask, pray and give thanks, pray and talk with me all the time. We should be in constant dialogue. You ask and I respond with suggestions and love and energies of all kinds. I always reply. I just don't do it for you. Think about how many people you have heard say that they prayed and asked me for something and sat for days or months waiting to be given whatever they asked for. It doesn't work that way. When you pray or direct thought to me, I always answer. I suggest things you can do to get your prayer answered the way you want, or answered in the way that might prove to be better for your soul growth.

> Do you remember the funny joke about the man who stayed in his house while the river by his home began to rise?

Yes.

> Then tell me how you remember it.

An old man, who considered himself very religious, lived in a two-story house alone. It began to rain and continued for days. The river began to rise almost to the road in front of his house.

A jeep came by and a ranger knocked on his door and said he was there to take the man with him before his house flooded. The man wouldn't go with him. He said, "God will save me." The river rose and flooded the first floor of his house and the man had to go to the second floor. A boat came by and someone yelled to the man to climb in the boat so he wouldn't drown, and they would row him to safety. The man again refused and said, "God will save me." The river rose higher and the man had to climb to the top of the roof to keep from drowning. A helicopter came by and let down a rope and told the man to climb up so they could rescue him. The man again declined and said, "God will save me."

The next thing the man knew he had drowned and found himself in heaven talking to God.

"God, I believed in you. Here I am dead. I prayed and prayed. Why didn't you answer my prayers and save me?"

God answered, "Well, first I sent you a jeep, then a boat..."

> That's close enough. Do you see what I mean? I send you jeeps, boats, helicopters, people, a thousand

things. You ignore them, waiting for me to speak and do it for you. It doesn't work like that. I speak in many ways. In fact, I really enjoy all the ways I try to talk to my loved ones. However, most of you have decided on the ways in which you will allow me to speak; and, you ignore the others.

It is good for you to pray and to remember what prayer is and to understand how it works. It helps you acknowledge a power beside yourself that can help you create what you desire. It helps you see that we are co-creators, acknowledging your creative abilities and mine as one.

When we created, we created with the gift of free will. It is an earthly law; it is a spiritual law. I cannot go against the gift I have given you. It is your greatest gift along with a chance to experience earthly life in various ways. Free will. You can choose whatever you want, whenever you want, in whatever way you want. I cannot go against that. I can, however, suggest easier, better and more direct pathways to the goal you desire to achieve. Just like a parent or a friend who cares, I do that because I love you and I want you to succeed.

How exactly do you know everyone of us personally, by name or what?

I know you by name and I can call you by name and I do. You have heard me get your attention many times by calling, "Anne." Although hundreds have the same name, even the same birth date, I know each of you individually, too. This is because each soul has their own special signature vibration, which can be recognized by all. It is so subtle that many of you incarnate cannot recognize it in each other; but those in the soul realm know everyone by the vibration emanating from them. Each hair is numbered can best be explained this way also. Within this individual vibration each organ, each hair vibrates in a particular way, and incarnated sensitive ones can feel and sense those vibrations. This is the way in which many work with healing, by sensing the vibrations out of accord, and directing energy to realign those vibrations. I am always aware of your soul vibration, its needs, its concerns and its joys; and since we are one, I am never apart from you either. I know you far better than you know yourself.

Countries have a particular vibration, which is a combination of all things in that country plus all their people. When masses of people change, even the vibration of a country changes. If, for instance, thousands of people change consciousness, it is enough to make major changes in a city or country. Then, if only one more person changes, it can tilt the scales, much like the hundredth monkey phenomenon and the whole city or country changes again. Therefore, one person can make a difference, a big difference. These changes can be spiritually good changes or changes that do great harm and damage to a city or country and to thousands of souls. Choose to be one that through your changes brings help, not harm, to others. Jesus did that, and his choices and pattern have impacted for good for thousands of years. Even though there is much misinformation about his life, much survived that is true and helpful. Seek out that knowledge if you would know yourself.

MESSAGES FROM GOD

CHAPTER 7

...God's revelations on... reincarnation, earth changes, prosperity, and healing the planet...

God, there are so many theories about reincarnation. What should we believe?

> Reincarnation isn't about believing or not believing. Reincarnation simply is. Whether or not you believe the soul returns again and again in different bodies, in many places, during various time periods, does not change the fact that it does.
>
> Reincarnation is an earthly law that is constantly in effect. You may not believe in electricity, but that does not stop the electricity. You may ignore the fact that radio waves exist, but they continue.
>
> I created all souls. These souls have been with me since that creation; and we have always been and will

always be one. Every soul was created with consciousness and awareness and in my image. Certain souls, with my permission or blessings if you will, chose to be part of a variety of experiences throughout the universes. Over eons of time many souls got caught up in those experiences and began to forget who they were. Some helped seed or populate the earth in life forms that evolved through the conditions of the planet. Others chose different places and also got caught up in the vibrations there.

Many loved these new and different experiences. Some got mired into energies they disliked. Since we were all one, we would meet and discuss their situations when their consciousness sought me out. The energies of these planets, stars, galaxies and universes were strong and the pull was great. Over time some souls would get so bound into whatever form they were experiencing that they forgot their way home to me. When the form they were using wore out, expired or dissolved, depending on where they were and the rules governing their particular place, their soul was free to return to me and to remember who they were. This could sometimes occur in months or years as time is now measured, or centuries and ages could pass.

Those who ventured to the mass which was called "Terra" for eons of time, and is now called Earth, were very creative and much of the beauty you see was because of that creativity.

What exactly do you mean by that?

> We had created together for eons. They had many powers at their disposal and could create the land, water and life forms, and did. They created the varieties of birds, fish, and animals. The story of Adam and Eve is symbolic, not literal, but there was an Adam. That's *another* story. However, these souls also interacted with souls elsewhere and there was travel back and forth, to and from many other places. Some of the created living life forms were exchanged place to place. You may notice some most unusual species, both those still living and those found in archeological digs from this exchange. The souls that set up residence on earth had the ability to breathe life into the animal kingdom, because the soul-life animals contain was not a soul such as theirs.

If it weren't you telling me this it would sound like something out of science fiction.

> You have heard that truth is stranger than fiction. Now you know.

Let me try to hang in there with you and make sense of this.

> Good, Anne. If you are to grow in understanding, you and others must be open to re-thinking old beliefs and considering new information.
>
> Over time there was much evolvement and chaos. The souls created forms that would enable them to experience all the energies of the earth. The human form developed, evolved and grew, and many souls became quite content in those forms. Those who weren't content returned to me. However, some souls literally

got trapped in the form, since it never died. There was no reproduction or death.

Many souls still with me, and those experiencing the earth met and discussed how best to handle the situation. Instead of spending hours telling you what we worked out, let me just say that from those meetings the earthly laws of reincarnation evolved. It was the best way to free entrapped souls from the forms they had created. But even more, it gave each soul a chance to experience earth-form, learn and grow, then when the form no longer served them, step from it and return to me. The soul could then decide if it wanted to return in another life form, go elsewhere, or remain with me. The division of male and female also began at that time, and reproduction.

I feel like I'm listening to a "Star Trek" episode. I have a thousand questions to ask you.

We have a lifetime for those questions, and I will answer each one for you in ways that you can best understand. Let me finish this right now, and we'll get to your questions later.

No soul entered an earthly form without first discussing it with me and with other souls and making plans. I gifted all souls with free will. What occurred and what is still occurring, is that the soul would enter the form, get so enamored with the feelings they experienced, that they would forget who they were, where their real home was, and what they had come in to do. Now, through its evolvement, you could call the form the earthly body. The spiritual laws governing the souls enabled them to still talk with me at any time. They were also able to meet with me when the form slept.

As time passed, the soul so layered each body with thought and energy that it became encased to such an extent that the soul became entrapped in it, and only communicated with me when the body was asleep.

Now, this is like a tiny condensed version of creation, which is inadequate I know; but it gives you a perspective and a foundation. For a long time the body lasted for hundreds of earth years because of the good environment, proper diet and lack of stress and pollution. Now the body seldom lasts a century; but was created to last much longer, and it still can if it is put in accord with earthly laws.

The soul returns to me fully when the body can no longer be used. You call this death. It is more correctly called the transition of the soul from the physical back to the spiritual. When the soul returns, we still have discussions, as from the beginning, about whether to return to another body when the vehicle and time are right, or to remain with me. I cannot go against a soul's free will. There is an on-going process of selecting, remaining, returning, and experiencing.

What about angels? Were those souls created in the beginning too, and do angels have souls like we do?

Some of the souls never left me; some manifested as angels, archangels, and other forms. Different laws govern these. For instance, when choosing to experience the angel forms, the soul is unable to ever return to forms on earth and experience that. They can create temporary bodies to use for short periods in order to do a work with humans. They can go elsewhere; but their vibrations can no longer be held in earth bodies. I know that many believe your dead become angels; but they do not in that form as such. They do return to being fully spiritual beings when they release from the body.

There are souls experiencing various forms in more places and more ways than there are fish in the ocean. Far more. It is always amusing when someone on earth is so adamant in asserting that there is no other life in the galaxy. That belief is like not believing in reincarnation. It does not matter that you believe there is no other intelligent life in the universe, or that there is no such thing as reincarnation. Life continues in the galaxy and souls return again and again.

Reincarnation is a troubling word for many. The connotations associated with it are often incorrect and anxiety producing. Let me explain how it works. There are no new and old souls. I created all souls at the same time. There are, however, souls for whom an earthly body is being experienced for the first time, although this does not happen all that often. Most souls have been on the earth plane for thousands of incarnations. They have incarnated as both male and female over and over again. They have experienced hundreds of time periods throughout the earth history. They have occupied hundreds, maybe thousands of different bodies. Souls do not inhabit animal forms. That teaching is called transmigration, and it does not exist in actuality. Souls of animals are not like the spiritual souls that take up residence in human forms. The vibrations of each are different. Neither would be in harmony in the other. Nor do souls evolve from rocks, through the animal kingdom to humans.

Remember we discussed that each time when a soul prepares to experience a new body, it meets with the parents, or mother if the father will not be in its life, and with the various relatives and friends that will be part of the incarnating experience. They discuss the mission they will plan to accomplish, their soul lessons and the interactions there will be with each. If after many meetings and discussions, the incoming soul and the parents and extended family feel they can make a commitment to the nurturing and strengthening of this soul, a covenant, an agreement is made between them all. Each commits to what they will do to help each other learn and grow, as well.

What happens if more than one soul wants the same body?

Very often many souls want to enter the same body. Helpers work with the souls to determine and help them decide which soul will be more suitable for the incarnation, or which soul can make the most growth.

When a determination is made, conception begins, and the sperm and egg unite and receive my touch. That is how that works. When the baby is born, the soul is released into the body at the first breath; and, it begins its new journey. At times individuals forget their commitments and covenants to the soul; and, things go awry. Some times the soul makes much progress and helps many along the way before returning to me.

When a journey is over, and the soul returns to me, the soul and its helpers discuss the incarnation, where the soul faltered and where it grew. There is an in-depth review of the incarnation and the soul determines whether it wants to prepare for another body or go elsewhere. It can also decide to rest for awhile. It can actually choose dozens of things to do or not do. So the laws of reincarnation do not make you return in a body. They do not require that you do anything, except become aware of yourself. Most souls choose to return. Not all do. Those who return do so for many reasons. They may feel they can do a stronger and better job if they return. They may feel they want to return and help loved ones who need their love.

Some may have made such progress that they want to return again and again to help those souls in earthly bodies who have forgotten who they are. Others may have done something so out of accord with their highest awareness, that they want to come back and set things right.

What about "walk-ins?" Those souls that enter an adult body and the other soul "walks out?"

We refer to these as soul exchanges. These are souls who do not want to or feel they cannot remain in a body; but they do not want to kill or destroy the body. Such a soul may meet with other souls; and, one of these may decide to enter the body when the occupying soul leaves. This does not happen that often but it does happen. Sometimes the soul occupying the body lets another soul enter who will do a work that the first soul feels unable to do. It is done very orderly; the memory bank of the occupying soul is absorbed by the entering soul. Much like downloading information into a computer. Usually the exchange is very meaningful and a good work is done on the earth plane through this.

Does this ever happen when the body is a child's or young person's?

Occasionally. Situations around the child would have to change drastically for this to occur, because the soul hasn't been in the body that long.

There are a few other things about souls entering new bodies that I will remind you of. The soul is not a baby remember, only the body is. Therefore the soul is always aware. Whatever is said or done around or to the baby by people who think it is unaware, imprints on the soul for that incarnation. Parents and family should be most cautious as to what the baby is exposed to in the way of pain, arguments, fighting and even violent movies. It does affect them in a less than positive way. Just as reading to the baby, touching it, loving it, talking to it with affection affects it in a positive way.

Sometimes the child seems to recognize or know a relative or friend and reaches toward them or responds to them in a special way. That is the soul recognizing another soul they have been with before. In any given family the incoming child may have been a mother or father to one of the parents, a grandparent to them, an aunt or uncle, or perhaps a teacher. They may have been brother or sister to their new brother or sister, a parent to them, a friend or teacher. You can watch the dynamics in the family and see a child trying to take over a parental role, or mothering a sibling. There may have been difficult or harmonious interactions in the most recent past life or ones further back.

How does karma work, and can you explain that a little more fully?

Karma means what you sow you will reap. Most people think karma is always something negative. They think if you killed someone in a past life, you will be killed in your current life. It doesn't work exactly that way. Karma is the earthly law of cause and effect. If you send out good thoughts, good thoughts will return to you. If you do some negative act, you will experience a negative act in return. Hopefully most of you will do far more good and good will be constantly returning to you.

Let's take murder. Perhaps your soul enters a body, incarnates, in a lifetime in the early 1800s. As you get older you make unwise decisions, forget who you are, and get mired in greed and anger. You then murder someone for their money and are never caught. You may live to be eighty and no one murders you and no one steals your money. It seems as if you got by with it, and are not held accountable.

When you die, you review that lifetime, your helpers advise you, and you see the great mistake you made and the many lives that suffered because of your act. You vow to do differently when you incarnate again.

You choose another lifetime in the late 1800s and someone breaks in your house and steals everything. You have the free will to be vengeful and angry and to try to find the person and spend years obsessing about your loss. Or you can choose to be angry and frustrated for a short period, forgive whoever stole your things, and pray for them. Your attitude about a given event determines the type of energy or karma you experience that lifetime and in future lifetimes. Something in you still remembers what you were taught and the vow you made in the time between lives; and, you choose the attitude that will help strengthen you.

Perhaps in that same lifetime someone kills a person you care about. You again have the choice as to how you will react to that situation. If you have compassion for the one that kills and begin to understand why someone might commit such an act, you begin to grow even more. It is then possible that with your change in consciousness and greater empathy and awareness, you may not need to meet the law of cause and effect by someone killing you. Or, you might choose to allow yourself to meet this karma in the same way you created it.

In actuality, the person I am describing had this very experience. In that same lifetime, he was held at gunpoint as someone robbed him. As the robber put the gun to his head to kill him when he didn't get enough money, he said to the robber, "You are a better person than this. You don't need to kill me. God loves you and I forgive you. If you are desperate for help, come home with me and I will feed you and give you more money there. Your mother and family would not want

> to see you this way." The robber lowered the gun, told him he was crazy, and ran off. His words caused the robber to rethink his life and ultimately turn his life in a better direction. The man's karma did not need to result in his life being taken, because of the wiser and more loving way he spoke with the robber.
>
> You can see that there can be thousands of scenarios depending upon the way a person has chosen to meet the law of karma and their willingness to change and grow.

I could almost see that whole thing in my mind. It sounds like there is a tapestry being woven around us and through us all the time, linking us with past lifetimes, karma, choices, love, you, each other. Sometimes we aren't aware and sometimes we are.

> Yes, it's very much like that. The earthly laws are fairly simple. The many scenarios interwoven in accord with earthly laws become more complex.

Is there a certain length of time you have to wait before you can incarnate in another body?

> The time between a soul leaving one body and entering another is as varied as individual bodies are. Some souls do not return in another body, as I have told you. Others review their life and are eager to get back in another body. They could enter in a few days or weeks after leaving their last body. Many spend what would be a year to a hundred earth years or more before returning. Frequently a soul will wait until the extended family of souls they were incarnate with leave

those bodies. They meet together and make plans to return as a group again. This is usually when the incarnation has been particularly enjoyable and productive, or when they wish to work with many lessons they left unlearned.

Many people have become discouraged when they hear or read that a person who commits suicide must stay in limbo until the time of their natural life ends. There is no limbo as such, nor would I require such a thing. A person who takes his or her own life has much the same experience that any soul has when returning. They review the incarnation and work with teachers and helpers to understand why they had felt there was no option but suicide. They determine whether or not to return in a body when they have learned enough lessons to strengthen them more fully. Certainly they have regrets about the act, and see that it solved no problems, only created more. The act ends that incarnation. Whatever good works could have been done by them can no longer be done. That is the most difficult thing the returning soul deals with. That and seeing their loved ones and friends grieving so badly.

Suicide is a great waste and loss, to the individual, the remaining family and the world. All the problems the soul did not deal with in that body will need to be met in the next incarnation. Often the circumstances will be less desirable than the previous incarnation.

Upon occasion, a soul is not quite ready to enter a body soon to be born. The soul is finishing a current incarnation, or for a variety of reasons the new body is ready too soon. The soul is not finished with its mission and cannot easily exit the current body. When a special soul mission can be better served by holding the new body and the soul continuing to remain for a short period of time in the current body, certain temporary "holding" souls enter for short periods of time. It can be for a few days or a few months, and rarely but upon occasion, for a few years.

The "holding" soul knows this is a temporary assignment; the soul that will enter later, knows that the body is being held until it can enter. The souls meet while the body sleeps and review what is happening. When it is time for the permanent soul to enter, the memory bank is transferred and the soul gets about its new mission. The "holding" soul also gets about its work. Usually the family unit around the baby is unaware consciously of what has transpired. They are all aware on a higher level.

This helps to explain why some children or adults, having true memories of their last lifetime, cannot get the dates to coincide, since in this incarnation, they were born in their current body before they died in their last lifetime. This is not as complicated as it sounds. Some researchers throw out valuable information a child remembers because of this. Again, it does not happen that often; but it *does* happen; and other religions have written about and know this.

That's amazing, God, but I *do* believe it. It makes sense about something that I read. In a book on children remembering past lives, the researcher did just that. He threw out a wonderful past life remembrance a child had, because when researching the past life, the man the child remembered being had not died before the child was born, but some time afterward.

– ✡ –

Do past lives as a male or female have anything to do with being attracted to a same sex partner this lifetime?

> It can. The attraction of two males or two females can be because of strong past life sojourns together. Other attractions can be because of past lives, also. Very often such attractions can cause a soul to get out of accord with what they came to do. Other times particular attractions can help free those who have made incorrect choices. It allows them to align with someone they find they are compatible with and whose spiritual ideals are the same. This is where it becomes complicated. Each soul must exercise its free will and make decisions it feels are best for its soul growth. No one else can judge such choices.
>
> Souls return over and over again with each other, in groups, even in communities. In any partnership of couples, the two may have had dozens of lifetimes, often many more, together. Some souls return together and marry when they could better meet their lessons in a relationship as friends or acquaintances. The marriage creates difficulties; the friendship would have been the better choice for all.

Why don't we remember our past lives?

>But, of course you *do*. You remember them as well as you remember events in the current lifetime. You have just been taught to suppress these memories and not trust them. Listen to very young children talk about when they used to be "big" and the details they share. Many parents, when hearing this, tell the child to stop making things up or ignore what the child is saying. The child gets the message that somehow it is wrong or it is irritating to their parent to mention such things. Or they think that what they have shared is of no value. For awhile they keep whatever they remember to themselves. Then from years of not having their memories acknowledged, they quickly take their thoughts somewhere else when these memories manifest.
>
>You constantly dream of past lives. Sometimes in the dream the characters are clothed in modern dress and yet are involved in activities from another time. I send you these dreams to remind you of who you are. You would not accept me telling you these things, so while you are asleep, I send you the information you wouldn't listen to any other way. There is always some key in the dream indicating it is information from a past life. Rusty locks, an old box, an ancient book, some piece of antique jewelry or decoration on a dress, are a few of those keys.
>
>The pictures that come into your mind are often scenes and memories of your past. You ignore most of this information, either thinking it to be your imagination or of little value. At any time you can wake up and

remember. For your soul remembers and your conscious mind longs for that same awareness.

I have heard people say they have enough to do *this* lifetime, they don't have time to look into any past lifetimes.

They have no idea of their loss by not doing this. You cannot know where you are going unless you know where you've been. This is something I have told many souls. Past life information enables you to know the strengths and weaknesses you have brought into this lifetime. It shows you relationship issues you have not resolved from the past. It enables you to see gifts you have developed that can be built upon in this lifetime. The study of your past sojourns is not a waste of time but a way to use your time more fully. It can keep you from making the same mistakes over and over. It can give you the courage to do something you have put off doing, when you discover you have done that thing quite successfully in your past lifetime.

Knowing yourself is a lifetime pursuit. You cannot truly know yourself unless you know your past lives. The awareness that your soul and all souls return again and again, makes you able to understand so much more about life, about others, and especially about yourself. You develop more compassion and kindness. You treat others like they were treasured family members. For they may have been such in your other lifetimes; and they certainly are on the soul level. You will discover, most of all, in seeking this self-knowledge, that it is a just and fair world and you are experiencing what you have either chosen or created.

From the time my youngest daughter, Debbie, was able to talk, she always acted like my mother, even telling me how to dress and comb my hair. It was so funny. I would tell her when she got bossy, "I'm the mother this lifetime. You're the child."

> And, as you began to remember, and listened to your dreams, you discovered she actually was your mother in your very last lifetime in the 1920s in New York.

Yes. I saw different parts of that lifetime in dreams, meditations, past life regression sessions, visions and from people who told me of their remembrances of being with me. I walked into a cathedral in New York City and heard a voice say I was married there. In a delicatessen in downtown New York, I had about ten minutes of an open recall of that life. It happened over a period of several years. I then checked old records in the library in New York to try and confirm some of the information.

> That's often how it works, a piece at a time, like a jigsaw puzzle until the picture is clear. At other times the memories come flooding through instantaneously. Sometimes a certain piece of music will open the floodgates of remembrance. Such music is my finger gently stroking the memories of your soul. Ancient objects you see in museums will also trigger your memories.

> Because you have been taught from childhood to ignore these memories, you will need to work diligently to open them up more fully. When you do, you will understand what an uplifting and transforming experience it is to know your real history. As you open the doors to your past, you will begin to open the other doors to your origin and to me.

Chapter 7

– ✡ –

There is never enough time to get everything done, God. It seems like time is passing by faster than ever before, or is this my imagination?

> Time, the hours, the minutes, the seconds are the most valuable commodities in a lifetime. More valuable than gold or diamonds. You have seen how rapidly time passes. In many ways you are delighted when a week is over and a weekend comes, but this fools you. In wanting a particular day to arrive, then another and another, before you know it an entire incarnation is over and you haven't done what you set for yourself to do. You excuse the time passing by assuring yourself that later you will do whatever it is you know must be done. Yet, you put it off for days and years and it isn't done, and you may then blame others. In truth you are responsible. Then instead of accomplishing your soul purpose, you discover that it is left undone. You die, then you wait for a body and return, and the cycle repeats itself. It is so common and so very sad for you, and wasteful.
>
> Time does seem to speed up the longer you are in an earthly body, until you release. This is true, especially, if you are working on things that you love and are busy in service to others. As a child there are times when an hour seems forever. As an adult a day seems a moment. So you are not imagining the feeling. Also, as you grow in wisdom you recognize that the years of an incarnation are coming to a close. You sense that there is something greater after you shed your

earthly form, but you have such joy being alive. Or, you have become so accustomed to being in that form that you don't want to let it go. Each moment becomes more precious then.

Others find themselves in such frail health or have let events so discourage them that they welcome the time of transition. For many of them time seems to drag as when a child.

The best way to make the most of time and to get done what is important to you is to schedule things, according to the priority you give them. As humans you often get distracted and are forgetful. It is not that the things that distract you are bad. They would be easy to identify if they were bad. Sometimes they are even good - a worthy effort as you call it - but they are distractions and they keep you from your real mission. These worthy efforts may cost you a wasted incarnation, weighed against what you set for yourself to accomplish. There are also disruptive forces, as I explained, that work in such subtle ways to distract you onto other less important things. Keep ever aware of such. C. S. Lewis wrote a very helpful book called *The Screwtape Letters,* to keep you watchful of such disruptive subtleties.

God, I just took my calculator and figured this out. There are 1,440 minutes in a day, 10,080 minutes in a week, 524,160 minutes in a year. In a 70-year lifetime there are approximately 36,691,200 minutes or 611,520 hours, not counting leap years.

Incarnated souls waste thousands of minutes and hours daily, weekly, monthly. Can you afford to waste *your* minutes or *your* hours?

I see what you mean. There are not that many hours or minutes in a 70-year lifetime.

> Eliminating clutter and simplifying your life will save thousands of minutes and hours over a lifetime. Taking care of yourself and your health gives you many extra minutes not spent fighting disease. This enables you to have more time for the things you enjoy and for the people you care about.
>
> The more simply you live, the more joy you have. The more you enjoy my creation, the less you worry and fret. Get outside in my glorious creation, not always inside in your heads, or inside in your offices and homes. Be learning, always learning, but learning with joy and having fun. Don't force children to have good grades but to find joy in learning.
>
> You actually have a lot of spare time. Dieters are encouraged to keep a record of everything they eat for a week, to see where they are fooling themselves. Keep a record of how you spend every hour for a week and you will see how much time you will find. All the things that bring you joy, that you insist you don't have time to do, you will find plenty of time for.

I never thought about doing that. I'll try it. I can see I waste a lot of time on trivia and seemingly worthy things that take me from what I know I am to do with this incarnation.

I realize I also get discouraged when I'm counseling someone and they don't follow my guidance. But, I don't always follow my own higher guidance or yours either, God.

It's easy not to. It takes more focus to do what you know to do for your highest good. Begin where you are but make haste slowly and divinely. Use time wisely and treasure it as a precious jewel. Setting priorities and balance is the key. Have some joy and play, rest and recreation, some work you find joy in, time to prepare and eat health-building food, time for planning and thinking things through, and take time daily for the reading of my words and other inspirational material.

Parts of the Bible can be inspirational if understood. Again, I will say that despite its mistranslations and errors, I spoke to many of my people, and some of it was recorded. I have also inspired others who would listen. Look for the inspiration in other's writings - not all is inspired. Some writings are not only uninspired but create depression, doubt and discouragement. Many that you have read are soul lifting. Choose those.

You must be watchful and let nothing prevent the next steps of the work you have come to do, lest in trying to help all, you fail to help any.

I am your rich father who gladly pours down upon you whatever you need, and whatever you ask. Let me help you each step of the way.

It seems like I ask you for help and many of those requests are denied.

Not denied my child. There is often the need to wait until the person requesting sets themselves in accord with the best within themselves, to use what they ask for in the correct way. Like de-cluttering your life. You see before this awareness of de-cluttering reached your consciousness, you would have added to the clutter when you had unlimited supply, even though some of it would have been used to help others. And acquiring more things would have severely limited your ability to serve and help others.

Material things are to be enjoyed. A home, car, clothes and furniture are to be used and enjoyed, not to take my place within the person's life. You have let yourself learn some fine soul lessons and removing clutter is one of them. But clutter is on so many levels as I have told you. Clutter clogs the mind, the body, the workplace, and the activities. Simplify. Simplify your life that you may be of greater service to your brothers and sisters. You can't help so well when all about you is cluttered and you continue acquiring. There is not time or space left for living fully. One can only drive so many cars, live in so many houses, wear so many clothes, and collect so many books.

Besides de-cluttering, order is important for all. You can remove clutter and still not have order. Any who say they work well in disorder and confusion fool themselves. Perhaps no other thing stifles creativity more than disorganization. Imagine what the universes would be like without order. Prepare for great things by attending to the little things, that the greater may be added. Don't be discouraged when you can't do it all at once. Remember, simplify one step at a time, never giving up, persevering and expecting to succeed at the goal you have set for yourself. Many have failed to fulfill their soul purpose because they got discouraged and quit before the race was over. Be not one of these.

As you do all things, do get wisdom for it is a great treasure. You *can* take that with you when you leave your body. Do not say you are getting wiser because you are getting older. Instead affirm that your wisdom grows from loving choices no matter what your age.

Let me paint you a word picture. See the whole earth as a giant computer and see a computer terminal for each person. Everyone is hooked up to the master computer, giving input and receiving input. All knowledge is available to everyone; but, you do have to learn your computer or you can only access a small part of the information available to you. You know how you had trouble learning how to pick up your e-mail; and, besides that you didn't even know what was on your laptop. You got too busy to check out your many programs and to use them.

I remember, and I still have various computer "opportunities."

Life is like that – people get so caught up in life that they don't even access or use what is so readily available to them. You know what happens when you have a problem on the computer, and you don't know what to do. So let's use the example as a metaphor that the life of each person is like a personal computer, and that God is like the major terminal to which all the PCs are hooked. All the angels have PCs too.

So what is the first thing you want to do? You want to read your instruction book, then experiment with what you read until you become more knowledgeable. You can take this further. Each time you are born you are given a new updated PC, but of course you don't get it without programs. In one program is the information about your past lives, relationships with people, everything you have ever done or said in every past life everywhere. All you need to do is to learn to access that information and you have all knowledge of yourself and the universe. Like the majority of people, you rarely become expert on your computer.

You know how you played Tetris the other night way past the time you needed sleep? That's what you do in life. You get off the track doing something and can't stop. That's all addictions are.

When you are spiritually uneducated, you suffer. When you work on a computer and don't know the simplest of commands, you suffer. It takes so much longer to understand and work out the problems. But, if you learn the program and practice, using a computer becomes much easier; and, next to the human mind is the greatest gift you can imagine to make life easier and more enjoyable.

— ✡ —

I'm confused about whether we should try to create wealth, save or invest our money, or give it all away to the poor. One book says one thing, another something else.

> Are you afraid of great wealth? Are you afraid it will change you? Are you afraid that the things that are so good right now might be lost? I tell you, they will not. Nor it wrong to expect great abundance and to allow yourself to create great abundance. I have told that to many others who have listened and written to share with all of you. This is an abundant universe and there is enough for all.
>
> The more you have financial stability and abundance, the more you can help and inspire others to create abundance, and the greater service you can be to others. Remove any doubt that it's not spiritual or not my will for you to prosper and have great material wealth, and prosperity of all kinds. Just commit to using the wealth in the best possible way to be of the greatest service you can possibly be. Use it to glorify your creation. Use it to help make other's lives easier, and to inspire them to help each other. Use it to have a joyful life.
>
> Anne, we have discussed some of the spiritual laws regarding fueling your physical body and extending your life. These earthly laws work without question. They always have and they always will. There is a powerful spiritual law that is distressful to most of you; but when it is practiced it allows for all kinds of em-

powerment and prosperity. It, too, always works. It always will. That is the spiritual law of tithing.

Tithing?

Yes, the awful "T" word. If the world understood tithing, there would be no poverty and all the research, all the healing, all the good that needs to be done to re-create this Garden of Eden – earth – would be accomplished. No one would die of starvation or thirst. No one. No one would be without a home. No one.

Tithing, as understood, means taking l0% of everything you earn and giving it to me. I don't need the money, but you need to tithe. This law enabled many Biblical and historical figures to prosper. The law regarding this is the acknowledging that there is always enough, and that in earthly bodies, you must be in accord with this earthly law of giving and sharing, if you would have all good come to you. For in giving, you create a vacuum, which can then be filled with even greater good. Without giving, there is no room for more good.

You are here on this planet, governed by a particular set of laws or energies, of which giving is one. When you give the "first fruits of your labor" to those who are currently less fortunate, it changes and empowers both you, the giver, and the receiver. The energies and vibrations from you and drawn toward you change. Being in accord with this law creates the prosperity that has alluded you. This prosperity is financial, emotional, physical, spiritual, relationships, love, health, and all good things you desire. Tithing does this by enabling a powerful energy to fill the space held by these gifts, and it frees the receiver to do more than just survive. It begins to free them to see that I am the source of all their supply and that they, too, must give to those even less fortunate.

How do you know that the money you're giving is being used correctly, and who do you give your tithe to when there are so many helpful organizations?

This is where your own inner wisdom and intuition come into play. First, give where you are most blessed or where you feel the organization is a blessing to others. Or, give where you believe your tithe could help a worthwhile cause grow and have greater outreach. Sometimes that is a church, sometimes a homeless shelter. Support the group or cause that you believe in. Do it with all your heart and soul, not grudgingly. For, the right attitude puts you in accord with this divine law. The wrong attitude negates the good that could have been done. Make your tithe the first check you write, the first coins or dollars you put aside, before bills, before luxuries. Put this spiritual law first, and everything will be added unto you.

That sounds familiar.

Of course, you have heard it and read it before. There is no new truth. All truth has always been and will always be. It is again before you, its presentation just changes.

Let me tell you a little bit more. Perhaps you desire to support organizations, because of the work they are doing, that are at some distance from you. Ask to be sent an accounting of how the money they receive is used and what percentage goes directly to the specific cause you are contributing to. Reputable groups will be glad to do this. Pray about it, ask me, listen for your inner guidance, and then decide where you want to offer your tithes.

If your intent is correct, even if an organization should ultimately fail to use the money in an ideal way, it will always serve some good because of *your* good intent. You may never know that; but I assure you it is true. You might decide to change where you are placing your tithe, based upon your feelings and what occurs. Ask me, I will direct you. In this way you will always stay aware and be a good steward of your supply.

If everyone were to give his or her 10% in this way, you would see a seemingly miraculous transformation of this planet. You would also find that 10% might not be enough for you to share, as you grow in awareness. I spoke to Malachi one day and told him of this earthly law: "Bring your tithes into the storehouse… and prove me now herewith, if I will not open you the windows of heaven and pour you out a blessing, that there shall not be room enough to receive it."

I have more to speak about this; but this is enough for now. Do you believe these things I have told you, Anne?

Yes, God, I do. Just a few more questions. Can you give parts of your tithe to dozens of organizations so that many will be helped? Also can you tithe your time instead of your money?

You can certainly give in that way but it is less powerful than giving the full amount in the way I have mentioned. Making a pledge, whether in writing, verbally or just to yourself, to support fully a helpful cause, is more powerful than small amounts of your tithe scattered and diluted to many causes. When you have larger amounts of money to tithe, enough could be given to help an organization make a difference in being able to implement worthy programs they have begun. Small amounts given to various organizations often keep a church or organization struggling along without making much progress. You will see the power that rises within you when you make such a pledge or commitment and follow through consistently. Again, I say to you, try it. Let me prove to you the truth of this spiritual law. I will help you with any questions you have.

You should tithe your time in service as well as your monetary supply. One does not eliminate or substitute for the other. Tithing is a sacred act; and, it benefits the tither far more than the recipient. Done with the right spiritual intent and from a loving heart, the benefits are on every level. Also, as you begin to prosper and create much abundance, if you have not tithed when you had a very limited income, you will find it much harder to tithe as you prosper.

Many teachers have theories about prosperity and tithing. Which things can we believe?

Some have listened to the leadings of my spirit. Among those are Catherine Ponder who wrote *The Dynamic Laws of Prosperity* and other helpful books about tithing and many other spiritual laws. Tony Robbins is another who accepted these insights and shares them well.

You will be amazed if you tithe consistently with a loving and giving attitude, how you will allow the riches of the universe to come to you. Hold each bill that you pay, each tithe that you offer in your hands and bless it. Ask that it blesses the receiver and returns to you a hundred fold or more. Try it. Test my promise.

For years predictions have been made about earth changes in and around the turn of the century. Is the earth going to shift on its axis and millions of people die? Will California sink into the ocean and the economy be destroyed?

> There are going to continue to be upheavals, but no catastrophic falling away of land like the state of California or New York. As long as the planet is abused, mistreated and scarred through greed, neglect and apathy, it will react with earthquakes and other upheavals in an effort to cleanse and heal.
>
> When you are sick, you react by releasing the poisons in your body through vomiting, diarrhea, and other expulsions. When you are toxic your skin erupts with rashes, boils and pimples. You cough, sweat, sneeze, and belch to release these toxins.

As soon as humankind begins to treasure their earth more, see it as a living entity unto itself as are they, and treat it thus, it will heal. This planet may not always continue, as many planets and stars have beginnings and ends; but, no time should be spent in trying to second guess when that will occur, and how, and trying to survive earth changes. It is not possible. You will waste this incarnation on planning for survival. Instead, spend the time doing whatever you can to help each other; and, remind each other who you are and who I am. Experience joy, not fear, while having the great gift of life on earth.

I can assure you, that despite your fears and what others have told you, this planet will not be destroyed, nor will the poles shift during the lifetime of any incarnate. There will be millions of you who will return a dozen times for centuries to come to this very earth. Take care of your earth, and your children's children's children will delight in it.

There aren't many places where you can grow as rapidly and have as much joy as on the earth. So delight in your sojourn and enjoy yourself fully. Think always of how you can help others. The grains and foods that thousands have stockpiled to "survive" would be better used to feed the hungry. The time spent in planning "survival" would be better spent in gaining self-knowledge and helping others.

The more your consciousness gets into a survival mode, the more paranoid most of you become. Think about the end result if there were earth changes. You could never be sure when those changes would occur. So, to be safe, you would have to stay near your stockpile all the time, or the changes could occur while you were somewhere else; and all that work would be lost. Or, if the shift of the poles occurred, do you really think that even those who have dug out underground caves and survival shelters would survive? Of course not. The odds would be worse than winning the lottery. To be really safe those who have constructed such would need to sleep in them 24 hours a day, just so they would survive in case the worst happened. Then think about what if you did survive and others, who had not stockpiled as you had done, began to starve. The children would cry at the entrance to your cave and beg for food and water. Could you turn them away? If you did, would life be worth living as you stepped over their dead bodies when you came out of your shelter?

A better way is to live your life so filled with love that you make each moment count in your soul development and growth. To learn all you can, for what you learn is never lost. To do all the good you can while you are incarnate. Then if there were earth changes, you would be ready to release the soul from the physical body and return to me. You have free will to choose to live in fear and stockpile to save your lives. What I have given you is a better way. Don't be afraid to "die." Fear only that you haven't lived fully and used the great gift of life as you chose.

Will we really be able to change the world and the consciousness of the world knowing all this?

Will you?

You mean will *I* do something to change things?

> Yes, will you? I remember you saying in a talk, "Someone should do something about this situation." Then, you said, "I realized I was that someone and it was up to me to do something."

I don't know exactly what to do on such a global scale.

> Begin where you are. Write letters to people in power, without anger, but with the strength and knowing within yourself that your opinion is important, could make a difference, and needs to be heard. Write your congressmen and women, your senators, your president, when it is needed and appropriate. Begin to tell the truth in all things, in every aspect of your life. Use part of your time to act locally, and do all you can to help in your corner of the world. First, act and choose to work on yourself, then help your family, then your neighbors. Treat each person as the holy soul they are. But always think globally. Let nothing cause you to lose hope. Eliminate doubt or fear. For how can you feel any of these things when I am working with you?
>
> When an official has been elected by majority vote locally or nationally, support that person in every possible way. It doesn't matter whether you voted for them or not. Look for the things you can agree with. Pray for them daily. Write them supportive letters, call and let them know you feel they are doing a good job. This is especially true of your world leaders, the president of the United States, and of each one elected to direct their particular country. You

are doing much damage in undercutting your leaders in every way. Before an election, different opinions can and should be voiced. But once the majority of the people have spoken, you would be wise to find the wisdom to support whoever was elected, and support them fully. If you do not, they cannot lead your country as well, and you will ultimately be the one effected by, and suffering from their limitations. Such a position of leadership is not only very difficult, such as you cannot imagine, but is a sacred trust between the leader and the people.

Any elected leader needs your loving support and prayers no matter what your political views are. The congress and senate do a great disservice to either party when they try to undercut and destroy the leaders they did not vote for. Try this and see how differently you feel when you just pray with unconditional love for all of your leaders. Pray that the very best of them comes forth from their soul for the highest good for their people and their country. You will be amazed at how you will feel and at the way in which you will perceive things when you do this. You will also often see remarkable changes in the leader as the prayer impacts upon them. When there is a crisis, pray even more diligently; and, ask and I will send a host of angels to these leaders. This is the better way.

Your consciousness and your thoughts effect everyone and everything, as do the consciousness and thoughts of each on the planet. When you feel you can't do anything else for a cause you believe in, pray. Pray without ceasing if you would heal your planet. I have told you that prayer works.

> Little changes you make in your thinking and actions, like what occurred in the l00th monkey story, can begin to make a difference globally. In essence, one person can make a difference. One changed person can so impact on others as to cause a chain reaction of good; and, that good can be felt throughout the whole world.
>
> You want to heal the planet? Heal yourself, help others and take one step at a time, making changes within and without. Each person needs to be needed and used, so they feel there is a place for them, and that they are contributing to something worthwhile. Begin to remember who you are. You are gods, children of mine, and you were created in my image. You are working on soul growth that will enable you while incarnate to do the things Jesus and the great masters have done, and greater things than these. The good you can do to help others on this planet is without measure; because, if you ask, I will aid you and there is nothing we cannot do together.

God I know you don't think of good and bad as we do, but doesn't it sometimes hurt you to see all the pain and suffering we put ourselves through on this planet, when it could be so much easier on us?

> What I see is the bigger picture. I know that ultimately you will stop hurting yourselves and remember who you are. It may happen in a minute or it may take a very long time; but one day I know you will come to yourselves and choose love over pain and heartbreak. I have given you the gift of free will until that day comes.

Chapter 7

I have a question I've heard many people ask. Where is earth on the spiritual or evolutionary scale, compared to other places in the universes?

> It is not at the bottom; but neither is it at the top. It could rise on the scale if enough of you who are incarnate began to awaken, remember who you are, let me guide you, and work together restoring and healing the planet.
>
> You must be watchful that nothing prevents the next steps of the work you have come to do, lest in trying to help all, you fail to help any.

Here I am having all these talks with you, God. It makes me feel good and I know if everyone would talk with you, how great they would feel, too.

> Yes, they would find that peace they seek. We have talked for years; but now you are working with our conversations in a new way. Bless Neale Walsch and those who have listened and shared what they heard. They gave you and hundreds like you permission to bring my words out of the dark into the light and share them with each other. Pray that hundreds and thousands like yourself will listen and share. How it's

shared is of little consequence. Someone may hand write a page of my words and share it with one or two people and it transforms their lives, or at the least gets them thinking in ways they hadn't before. Someone like Neale may write a best seller, it touches millions of lives, and these souls begin to remember who they are. See numbers aren't important. And, now the fact that you want to listen to me and agreed to get my guidance out to others, whatever that takes, is exactly what your soul came in to do.

God, it's been a good day. All is well in my corner of the world. I know all is not well in other corners of the world. I desire to enjoy my corner without guilt; but I also want to bring light into other corners that are now in darkness. I thank you for the wisdom and guidance you have given me all my life. Now I ask you to help me as I get our book together.

Hello, my dear Anne. We did have a great day, didn't we? Yes, it is dark in many corners of the world. You have a candle right now. While you have a candle, use it well and share your light with those who have none. One day you will have a light that never burns out, to help illumine those corners. When you exchange the candle for that light, you will bring even more light to this world. Use both wisely, but *use* them. Do not keep their light for yourself.

Do you remember the story of the man who led many down the stairs of a building when the lights went out in NY, with just the light from his wristwatch? That is a case of using whatever light is available to you to light the way for others.

That makes the point, God. I understand. I'm glad I have a candle.

Anne, do not worry at all what others think or say about you. For most people, both men and women, falter because of this. No one can judge but a very small part of the soul that you are. People make a 100% judgment on the 1% they perceive of you and each other. Yet, often you let others' judgment affect you adversely and cause you to doubt or falter. You think that their mistaken small judgment is how you really are. Think again on these things. For you, too, judge others the same and forever see them 100% the way you perceive them, when they are only 1% that way. When you look at others and they look at you as the souls that you are, then the planet begins to heal.

I need many of you for the healing this planet requires to sustain the creation of all. You are one; be glad there are many. I wish all souls alive would remember that they can talk with me and hear me; but many will not. Not this time.

God, what do you consider your greatest messages to us?

Live life so fully and so well and in such an awake state that you miss no opportunity to serve, no opportunity to have joy in its fullest. When the form no longer serves its purpose, you step from it anticipating the greatest joy and journey of your life. This is your life as it was meant to be lived.

All things are easy when we share the load. There is nothing we cannot do. Go forth and love others. Build treasures in heaven. Joy in my garden Earth and treat her lovingly and tenderly so that future generations may enjoy her gifts and beauty.

You want to move a mountain? Nothing to it if you believe. You cannot do it alone; but, with my help, we can move mountain ranges and we *have*.

We have moved mountains?

Yes. In the dawn of time, when the morning stars sang, as we created together. When we worked and were as one. We all created then. You simply took leave and forgot for awhile. It is time to awaken and return to me.

Remember that I love you and that I call each of you by name. Will you answer my call and let us again create together a heaven upon this earth? Come, I will remind you and show you how.

I will speak with you whenever you ask - anytime, anywhere – always.

Will you listen?

ACKNOWLEDGEMENTS

The messages in this book have come from years of my conversations with God, our on-going dialogues, my questions, and his answers. I am deeply thankful for these moments of awareness in his presence. I am also thankful for so many friends and family who were excited and enthusiastic about these messages and encouraged me to continue listening.

No one has been more supportive and excited about my conversations with God than my husband Herb. And no one has ever loved me more. Thank you sweetheart for bringing such laughter, fun and happiness into my life, and for being such a kind and loving husband, father and grandfather. I have learned so much from you. It is such a blessing to be married to you and to work together in a work we love. I adore you.

I have three children whom I love deeply: Bob, Andrea and Debbie. I am so proud of each of you and especially glad you chose me to be your mother. Thank you for loving me despite the many mistakes I made raising you. Stephen is my son in the spirit plane, who died at 15. I wish he were here with us; but I am thankful for the years we had with him and that our love and communications continue.

I am so blessed with my grandchildren, Melissa, Rob, Vanessa, and Krystalyn. I am thankful they have all lived near us since they were born and we got to grow up together. Now, Melissa is in the Navy in Washington State, Rob at Harvard, Vanessa at Arizona State University and Krystalyn, a lively teenager, who just made the varsity cheerleading team. They know how much I love them. There is an adorable toddler named Chance and his three brothers who live in Washington State that I claim as my grandchildren, too. They are being lovingly raised by my daughter Andrea and her partner Tami. They don't know how much I love them; but I would correct that if we lived closer.

I'm thankful to have Arlene Puryear, Ph.D., Herb's daughter, in my life; and also Herb's brother Bill. After being certified in Scuba, I had my first dive in Hawaii with Bill until Herb could join us. Our dive mates asked me if Bill was my husband, the famous Italian movie star. He liked that. My brother, sister, nieces, nephews and their wives, husbands and children are a blessing in my life, also. I don't see them nearly enough.

The Logos Center, where many of us work and volunteer, is a non-denominational church and center for holistic healing and education. We founded Logos in 1983, based on the Great Commandment: Love God with all your heart, mind and soul, and love your neighbor as you love yourself.

I have been so blessed and surrounded with wonderful friends who care, who forgive me when I'm a turkey, and encourage me when my faith falters. I am fortunate to be working side-by-side with so many truly good people, in a work we love.

I want to acknowledge and thank a few of the wonderful people in my life: Dennis Linehan, who has been there for me during the best and worst of times, with a loyalty and friendship that has blessed my life; Elizabeth, his wife whose caring has been such a gift; and Peg, his mother, a dear and loving friend; Stephanie and John Schroeder, who make me take time to play and let me be me. They taught me to be the dog-lover I have become by the way they love Murray and Sylvia; Bill Roberts, with whom I have laughed and cried and shared so many years of work and friendship;

Doris Rapp, M. D., one of those loving souls, with a pure heart, who is making a difference in the world, and who is responsible for my daily joy of having dogs; Pat Hughes, from whom I have learned so much and who lovingly helps in every way, unconditionally; Mari & Bob Messinger, whose heavenly music lifts my spirits always, their lovely daughter Heather and Mari's delightful mother, Kari Gordon; Sam, Sue and Jenny Rose Buford, who inspire me with their service; Katie Pushor, whom I admire greatly for her many talents and zest for life; Pat Druckman, who has been such a faithful and supportive friend; Rev. Jeanne Davis, a truly caring and helpful soul; Linda Wagner, filled with light and goodness; and Linda Manning, who radiates love to me and everyone she meets, sometimes with her angel-dog Snickers tucked under her arm.

To the other members of our Thursday night study group who pray, meditate and listen to God each week and will one day share their messages too, I am thankful for what each of you adds to my life and understanding: Rev.Beth Donnell, who works lovingly wherever and whenever she is needed, ditto her husband, Bob; Al McRae, who watches over us and our work like a Guardian Angel; David Stipes, a soul-brother from the moment we met; Doodie and Ted Trimbur, whose healing spirits makes life so joyful; Bill Risley,Sr., D.C., who keeps us all "healed" with his magic touch and humor; Tahna Maree, who inspires us with her art and who transcribes the group's messages from God; Mary Thornton, whom I admire and love being around; Jacqueline Alexander, who inspires me with her inner work and guidance; and Jana Tuggle, another soul sister.

I am so thankful to God for friends and fellow seekers like Shirley Wade, Glenda Myers, Jo Addah and Gene Watson, Nan Terry, Barbara and Ed Balch, Joe Hornback, D.C. and wife Kim, John Liebl and wife Rose, Bill Risley,

Jr.,D.C. and wife Amy, Rev. JoAnne Copeland and Stephanie Valencia, Jay and Leilani Dikkers, Mary Greenberg, Lisa Glaze, Angela Schumacher, Doris Heath, Jinny Kay, Edye Levinson, Marie Drift, Barbara Rickli, Diane Maxwell, Betty O'Shea, Ray Kopman, Ernie Wheeler, Harry and Anne Smith, Debra Kennedy, Ian and Debra Smith, Alice Marie, Sherri Reuss, Lidia Runge, Marva Ibarra, Donna Brown, Heather Moeller, Diana Mondeau, Roxanne and Rick Snyder, Kay Diego, Darlene and Cindy Sanner, Lynnda Bartlett, and Mina and Bob Lopez.

I am deeply appreciative of my wonderful and energetic agent Gail Hochman, who hangs in there with me; Julie Rubenstein, former executive editor at Pocket Books, Simon & Schuster, who got *Stephen Lives!* published; Jean and Bill Tiller, Elizabeth and Joe Chevola, Richard Gerber, M.D., Marge Risley, Lou Wilson, Jamie Abersold, Kay Gee, Pat Suemoto, Susan O'Hata, Kelsey Sears, and Terri Baltes, D.C., Marj and Jim Short, John Walsh, Cynthia Griffiths, Daphne Shelton, Lou Diekemper, Carol Marie Weiss, Loren and Judy Garretson, Lynn Thompson, Carol Compston, Grace Longo, John and June Brookshire, Dennis and Glennda Gilmour, Joe Gilmour, Daphne Starr Bush, Connie Weber, Barbara King, Jessee van Schoonhoven, Cec Storer, Frank Tribbe, Kathryn Woolway, Ron Alexander, Candace Weiss, Andelka Cek, Bette MaCrae, Susanna Neal, Debby and Roger Cason, Maisie Marven, Nancy Glass, Lucy Wornson, Ed and Arlene Holcomb, Barbara Cefalu, Rev. Margaret Brown, Bernice Wilson, Marion du Maurier, Grace Fogg, Yon Y.Lee, Elva Wing, and Sudi Walworth.

And special thanks to my dear third grade teacher in Danville, Kentucky, Elizabeth Doolin, now of Harrodsburg, Kentucky, for her friendship. She has shared her memories of me, my family and schoolmates, that would otherwise have been lost to me forever.

Blessings and love to my dear friend Ruth Montgomery whose book *Search for the Truth* changed my life forever. There are so many of you in the Logos community of friends to thank – so many people in Phoenix and throughout the country...and the world...who labor individually and together to make the world a better place. You have kept this work going forward over the years, prayed and meditated, lovingly sacrificed every step of the way, enabled Logos to build a new home, helped in dozens of other ways, and done it all with love and caring. You are all truly making a difference. God knows who you are. And, I know who you are.

I'm getting more and more friends and family in the Spirit Plane: Al McRae's lovely mother Marj Humphries, one of those lights whose death dimmed our corner of the world considerably; Olga Roberts, Bill's mother, whom I grew to love; Dorothy Drew, my intuitive friend who shared her helpful guidance for years; a dear friend Charlotte Roberts, who fought a valiant battle and never lost hope; Marie Kleyn, a truly loving soul; Ray Diekemper, whose love and service helped so many; Mary Grone, Regina Marshall, and Nan Heral, all lights to this work; Bob McIver, our long-time faithful and reliable friend; the Lubbock Puryears who lived their faith; my kind and loving father, Stephen Smith; and Virginia Ryder, my beloved friend who died but still keeps an eye on me. They probably *all* do, I feel them around - a *lot*.

I want to acknowledge the unconditional love my Mother gave me all my life. I was with her when she died several years ago. Those hours forever changed my understanding and removed any fear I had of being around dead bodies, or avoiding funerals and open caskets. I was aware of being part of the cycle of life, birth and death, beginnings and endings, eternal life. I will always be thankful for that gift. I miss her. I found several messages she left me, saved on my answering service, so I can hear her voice every few months, reminding me how much she loved me...and still loves me.

I can't imagine life without lovable Beethoven and energetic little Happy, our male toy poodles. They love us unconditionally, and keep us smiling and laughing every day with their playfulness. I used to make fun of the way people spoiled their pets. I have become the worst. But, they *are* the smartest, cutest and sweetest dogs... (See what I mean?). Karma!

And, thank you God for modern technology – especially my computer.

I did not capitalize any pronouns or most words relating to God. He is our friend. We are not separate; he is not *out there* and we are *here*. We are *one*.

It is the love for my family and friends and the love God has poured out upon me, that helps me keep trying to be a better person. I continually ask God for direction on how to be a better wife, mother, grandmother and friend and to accomplish what I came in to do with my life. That I don't always follow his guidance, is not *God's* fault.

I can't imagine not talking with God. I can't imagine God not answering me. I hope that each of you will find the joy that comes from daily talks with God, and keep a journal of his messages to aid you on your journey.

Love and blessings,
Anne Puryear

TALKING WITH GOD: A SHORT HISTORY

One of the truly wonderful things that has happened in our time has been the extended appearance on the list of best selling books of *Conversations with God,* by Neale Donald Walsh. Imagine it! Someone in these times claiming to talk with God! Consider further that millions of these books have been *sold* and *read* with enthusiasm.

The truth is, if we consider the Hebrew Bible or the New Testament to be "Conversations with God", this type of 'book' has *always* been on the list of "best selling books." As a matter of fact, it is *the* best selling book of all time. This is a wonderful thing too!

However, humankind has had more than a few problems with the claims that certain texts and scriptures were divinely inspired. On the one hand, there have been those "bibliolators" who have deified the Book itself claiming that their King James Version or their Torah or their Koran contains the full extent of the "Conversations with God" that may ever be received. Most of these people are "authoritarian" personalities who are seeking "Authoritative" answers. On the other hand, there are those naysayers who think that even if there were a God, such a Being would never deign to speak to humankind.

Nevertheless, we have the very widespread occurrence and acceptance of the fact that God speaks on occasion through "inspired" human channels. If we take the sixty-six 'books' of the Christian Bible as an example, it seems that God really likes to talk. Some say he talked for a 2000-year period; but for the last 2000 years he has talked no longer because He has said all He has to say. Yet, we have not only the canonical texts of the major religions; but, also there have been, over the centuries, many who have reported on their direct encounters and conversations with God. It seems indeed that God still has a special propensity for conversation. We may in fact add to the long list of names given to this Being and think of 'Him' as 'He Who Likes to Talk.'

In truth, it seems that He will talk with *anyone who will listen*. The rarity of this phenomenon is not because He is so disinclined to speak but rather from the unfortunate fact that there are so few individuals who will take the time to attune, listen, record and report on what they have 'heard.'

Anne Puryear has been one of those rare souls who has over the years been willing to practice these four steps: attune, listen, record and report. And, she has reported for years, actually since she was a child, that she talked to God and that He responded and she could hear and understand what He had to say.

If we accept the fact that sane people talk to God and that they and others may be enriched by what they receive, then we may rediscover a very rich heritage of 'Conversations' going back to the very beginning with Adam and Eve. This first recorded conversation also gives us a hint about problems for subsequent conversations. In the book of Genesis we are told of Adam's first words to God: "I tried to hide from you because I was afraid." This statement reflects the sad plight of humankind, even to this day. We don't confront Him face to face because we are afraid. Then, we don't feel 'worthy.' In fact, we are not 'worthy' but for the greater part, He has settled for using "unworthy" channels. As a loving father, He sees only the good in us, anyway.

Even so, there have been those bold ones over the centuries who have encountered and reported on their conversations with this One Who Likes to Talk. In every age and from every religion great but rarely appreciated mystics have emerged who have encountered the Divine and in turn quickened the hearts and souls of their followers.

The universality of these Encounters leads us to a second fear: What if what God says to one person does not match exactly with what He says to another? Should we choose one and throw out the other? Is one right and the other wrong? Perhaps rather we should look for a growing clarity in our own understanding.

Properly regarded, the Bible itself is a continuing upgrading of the understanding of what God was trying to say to his people. Some Jewish scholars have commented upon and properly taken pride in the growth of the understanding of God's purpose with humankind that is reflected in the changes in consciousness from the first five books on through the growing awarenesses of the prophets. For example, in the earlier days, there were the animal sacrifices. The later prophets heard God say, "I take no pleasure in your burnt offerings." The important thing about these 'upgrades' is not that God has changed His mind; but, rather, that we have grown in our understanding of His true spirit.

We are most likely to have a problem with the notion of 'conversations with God' when we look for theological statements that are doctrinally consistent with what we think God 'ought' to say. The truth, I think, is that God is not a Theologian. He is a Lover. He may not even want us all to have the same ideas. The setup in this earth plane experience surely predisposes us to have vastly different backgrounds and experiences; the inevitable outcome is that different peoples have different ways of thinking.

It is rather that He wants us to have the same ideal, which is very simply, love. We are to love both those whom we esteem the most and those whom we esteem the least. He is most interested in love and His communications are about love. He wants most of all to speak to us, his children, of His love for us and to call us to the way of love with our brothers and sisters. We will hear Him most clearly when we listen for the language of love, for He told us, thousands of years ago, "I have loved you with an everlasting love."

In our own time there was a great soul, Edgar Cayce, through whom many felt God spoke directly. Yet, even some of his greatest admirers hesitated to put him in a class with, say, Jeremiah or Obadiah because they were in the Bible. Nevertheless, if you read these sources and compare them within your heart to see which one most nearly meets the criteria of helpfulness and hopefulness, your spirit may answer with His spirit as to the 'inspiration' of the Cayce material and to other recent sources. After all, should not one of the measures of true 'inspiration' be the extent to which the text 'inspires' the reader?

Once Cayce was asked, "What is the highest possible psychic realization?" His Source replied, "That God the Father still speaks directly to His children, even as He did in the days of old." This was given not to just a select few but to all of us. Thus, I do not hesitate to affirm that God still speaks. Two wonderful little books illustrate some of these contemporary sources. *God Calling,* edited by A.J. Russell, and *Opening Doors Within,* by Eileen Caddy are self-authenticating messages from God. On every page the contemplative reader is guaranteed to find an 'inspired' message that will lift the spirit. And, who could have loved God more than the great Yogananda? Surely his writings are 'inspired' by God.

Anne Puryear, also the author of *Stephen Lives,* in which she reports on her conversations with her son the spirit plane, is a "listener" who regularly records what she hears. For more than twenty-five years Anne has had and has worked with a 'gift of the spirit' like that of Edgar Cayce. For more than eighteen of these years, I have conducted the spiritual counseling sessions she has given for thousands of people. Before every one of these sessions, I have said a prayer asking God to speak directly through her to those seeking help. I believe that He answered these prayers and that He has spoken to those who came in sincerity seeking aid for a genuine need. The 'Conversations' continue!

Did Moses and Micah and Edgar Cayce and Yogananda and Eileen Caddy and Neale Donald Walsh and Anne Puryear actually hear God? Perhaps we can best think of them as pioneers who have brought us all a step closer to a willingness to become "listeners" ourselves. Have we not always known that He speaks to us in that "Still Small Voice" that comes from within ourselves? Then, let us all become 'listeners.'

In the meantime, we have much to learn from these great pioneers and from the messages they have received and so courageously made available as 'gifts' to us. And now we have before us this new and exciting gift, *Messages from God*. Read it as you would enjoy a great feast with new and delicious dishes at a banquet; let your mind be opened to wonder, let your heart be filled with love, let your spirit be lifted with hope, and let your soul be freed to soar.

Herbert Bruce Puryear, Ph.D.

SCRIPTURES, QUOTATIONS AND EXCERPTS FROM WRITINGS ABOUT GOD

THE HEBREW BIBLE

In the Hebrew Bible, God speaks to:

> Adam, Eve, the serpent, Noah, Abraham, King Abimelech, Jacob, Moses, Balaam, David, Solomon, Hosea, Jonah, Isaiah, Ezekiel

> God speaks to 15 in all.

Numbers 11:29

> *And Moses said unto him, Would God that all the Lord's people were prophets, and that the Lord would put his spirit upon them!*

Jeremiah 31:34

And they shall teach no more every man his neighbour, and every man his brother, saying, Know the Lord: for they shall all know me, from the least of them unto the greatest of them, saith the Lord.

Isaiah 43:1

God has called you by name.

Ezekiel 6:1

And the word of the Lord came unto me...

Proverbs 3:6

He will always guide you

Kings 3:5-13

The Lord appeared to Solomon in a dream by night; and God said, Ask what I shall give thee. And Solomon said...Give therefore Thy servant an understanding heart...And God said unto him...I have done according to thy words: lo, I have given thee a wise and an understanding heart...And I have also given thee that which thou hast not asked, both riches and honor.

Jeremiah 29:13

And ye shall seek Me, and find Me, when ye shall search for Me with all your heart.

— ✡ —

THE HOLY BIBLE
NEW TESTAMENT

Luke l: 37

With God, all things are possible.

Romans 8:39

You cannot be separated from God's love.

Hebrews 13:5

God will never leave you or forsake you.

Revelation 3:20

Behold, I stand at the door and knock: if any man hear my voice, and open the door, I will come in to him, and will sup with him, and he with Me.

St. Luke 18:27

The things which are impossible with men are possible with God.

II Corinthians 6:16

Ye are the temple of the living God; as God hath said, I will dwell in them, and walk in them; and I will be their God, and they shall be my people.

Hebrews 8:10-11

For this is the covenant that I will make with the house of Israel after those days, saith the Lord: I will put my laws into their minds, and write them in their hearts: and I will be to them a God, and they shall be to me a people.

And they shall not teach every man his neighbour, and every man his brother, saying, Know the Lord: for all shall know me, from the least to the greatest.

— ✡ —

THE HOLY BIBLE

THE ANCIENT EASTERN TEXT FROM THE ARAMAIC OF THE PESHITTA

Psalms 82:6

You are gods; all of you are children of the most High.

Proverbs 2:3-6

If you cry after knowledge and lift up your voice to understanding, if you seek it as silver, and search for it as hidden treasure; then you will understand how to worship the Lord and find the knowledge of God.

Isaiah 40:8

The grass withers, the flower fades; but the word of our God shall stand for ever.

Jeremiah 29:13

And when you shall seek me with all your heart, you shall find me, says the Lord.

John 14:12-13

Truly, truly, I say to you. He who believes in me shall do the works which I do; and even greater than these things he shall do...

Whatever you ask in my name, I will do it for you...

John 16:13

When the Spirit of truth comes, he will guide you into all the truth; for he will not speak from himself, but what he hears he will speak; and he will make known to you things which are to come in the future.

John 16:15; 17:28

I have always called you friends, because everything that I heard from my Father I have made known to you.

I came forth from the Father and I came into the world; again, I am leaving the world and I am going to the Father.

Matthew 3:16,17

When Jesus was baptized, he immediately went up out of the water; and the heavens were opened to him, and he saw the Spirit of God descending like a dove, and coming upon him;

And behold a voice from heaven which said, This is my beloved Son, with whom I am pleased.

I Corinthians 3:16

Do you not know that you are the temple of God, and that the Spirit of God dwells in you?

James 1:5

If any of you lack wisdom, let him ask of God, who gives to all men liberally and with grace, and it will be given him.

James 3:17

The wisdom that is from above is first pure, then full of peace, and is gentle, obedient, full of mercy and good fruits, without partiality and without hypocrisy.

2 Chronicles 18:4

And Jehosophat said to the King of Israel, inquire I pray, for the word of the Lord today.

OPENING DOORS WITHIN

Eileen Caddy

In l953 Eileen Caddy of the Findhorn Foundation in northern Scotland first began to receive personal guidance from a still, small voice deep within her, from a source she calls the God within.

All you need is deep within you waiting to unfold and reveal itself. All you have to do is to be still and take time to seek for what is within, and you will surely find it.

Inspiration and intuition come from within. Let your learning come from within. It is not wasting time to be still and wait upon Me. We are one. I AM within you. Start the day by giving thanks. My blessings are being poured down upon you all the time.

Do you believe that you can walk and talk with Me? When you recognize me in everything and call upon Me and seek My help, everything starts to fall into place in your life.

— ✡ —

GOD CALLING: A DEVOTIONAL DIARY

In England, two women were facing a hopeless future and then He spoke. And spoke again!

You Shall Know: Walk with Me. I will teach you. Listen to Me and I will speak. Continue to meet Me, in spite of all opposition and every obstacle, in spite of days when you may hear no voice.

As you persist in this and make a life-habit of it, in many marvellous ways I will reveal My will to you. You shall have more sure knowing of both the present and the future. But that will be only the reward of the regular coming to meet Me.

To the listening ear I speak, to the waiting heart I come. Sometimes I may not speak. I may ask you merely to wait in My Presence, to know that I am with you.

— ✡ —

CONVERSATIONS WITH GOD, BOOK I

Neale Donald Walsch

I have heard the crying of your heart. I have seen the searching of your soul. I know how deeply you have desired the Truth. In pain have you called out for it, and in joy. Unendingly have you beseeched Me. Show Myself. Explain Myself. Reveal Myself.

I am doing so here, in terms so plain, you cannot misunderstand. In language so simple, you can't be confused. In vocabulary so common, you cannot get lost in the verbiage.

So go ahead now. Ask Me anything. Anything.

Listen.

I will speak to you if you will listen. I will come to you if you will invite Me. I will show you then that I have always been there.

— ✡ —

THE EDGAR CAYCE READINGS

<u>*Reading 900-254:*</u> *in the year 1926:*

A prominent Jewish businessman from New York, Morton Blumenthal asks a question and requests advice about his conversations with God:

I am now writing, or have been writing what I call "God Speaks to Clem..."

In a trance state reading Edgar Cayce advises: Keep it up – very good. It would win the prize with the Atlantic Monthly... Ladies Home Journal... with any of those.

In a 1934 lecture Edgar Cayce said: It once bothered me a great deal as a child that God spoke to the people in the Bible and did not speak to us. Now I believe that he does and will speak to us if we will only listen. We build barriers between ourselves and God.

In the following numbered spiritual trance readings through Edgar Cayce:

<u>5752-02:</u> God speaks rather to EVERYONE! Whosoever will may learn of him.

God speaks to man, even as man seeks to

commune with Him. He has made thee to be a companion with Him.

3018-1: To WHOM does the Master of the Way speak? To THEE. To THEE!

God speaks to those who seek His face, who seek His ways.

900-328: ...that men might know there is the God in Israel as speaks to men ... in the way that brings joy, peace, understanding, to all peoples.

900-330:. ...God the Father speaks to Himself through man and man's activities in the earth. The spirit is of the Father and all force is of God.

When God speaks, the command must be obeyed... the entity gives self as ready to be commanded, as in the inner self, or God speaking to the entity through self.

1646-1: As the guardian angel is ever before the face of the Father, through same may that influence ever speak.

CALL OF THE SPIRIT

Merritt Horn

Who told you that my revelation had ended? that having spoken I would speak no more?

I tell you that I shall speak to my children as they have need of me. I shall not withhold my spirit from any of them, for I hear their cry and I shall answer.

It is good that you search the records for my message, but you should not think that I speak from them only, for my spirit lives within you and I speak to you always. You know this in your heart. Listen then to the spirit. Let go of your small illusions; reach for the greater realities.

HOW YOU CAN TALK WITH GOD

Paramahansa Yogananda

Talking with God is a definite fact. All of you may communicate with Him; not a one-sided conversation, but a real talk wherein you speak to God and He responds.

For in God lies the answer to every desire of the heart.

— ✡ —

THE HOLY MAN AND THE PSYCHIATRIST

Sai Baba

One of the first principles of living is the practice of silence. For the voice of God can be heard in the region of your heart only when the tongue is stilled and the storm is stilled and the waves are calm. Silence is the speech of the spiritual seeker.

In that state of bliss...one thinks God, breathes God, lives God.

See all thoughts as God. Then, only God-thoughts will come. Seek God in the depths of yourself.

— ✡ —

... thus saith the Spirit of God through many sources

The Arcturian Connection

The soul that talks with God may feel a special affinity for the vastness of the night sky and especially for Arcturus. The handle of the big dipper points to the star Arcturus. Arcturus is in the constellation Bootes, The Herdsman, or we might call it the Shepherd. It is 37 light years away and is one of the closest bright stars to us. The Bible tells us of a time, "when the morning stars sang together and all the sons of God shouted for joy." Job 38:7. In the same chapter, we are told of "Arcturus and his sons." Job 38:32. Perhaps the joyous sons of God are indeed "the sons of Arcturus."

Edgar Cayce tells us that "Arcturus, the wonderful, the beautiful," may be called the center of this universe and is the central force from which entities may come into the earth. And this is the way, the door, out of this system for which there may be the entrance into other realms of consciousness. Arcturus represents a glorious state of consciousness. The symbol of Arcturus is two overlapping equilateral triangles, as seen in the great symbol known as the Star of David. Jesus entered through Arcturus, the gateway to this solar system, as did many of us, and all will exit through this gateway when completing our earthly sojourns. For some of us, Arcturus is *home*.

Anne Puryear invites you to write her and share your conversations and messages from God.

For more information on books, tapes and videos, to receive a free copy of the quarterly *Logos Journal,* with articles by the Puryears, including Anne's column, *Messages from God,* write or call:

The Logos Center
P.O. Box 12880
Scottsdale, AZ 85267-2880

Phone: 480-483-8777

FAX: 480-483-8494

Orders: 1-800-737-9620

Visit our website: www.logoscenter.org
email: email@logoscenter.org
Visit our online bookstore: ecayce.org

ORDER FORM

MAIL TO: New Paradigm Press
P.O. Box 12880
Scottsdale, AZ 85267-2880

Phone, orders only: 1-800-737-9620
FAX order to: 480-483-8494

Please send_____copies of **MESSAGES FROM GOD.**
I am enclosing $17.95 per copy ($17.95 x no. of copies) _____

Plus postage and handling:

    Orders to $50 – $4.95 postage and handling _____

    $51 to $99 – $9.95 postage/handling _____

    $100 or over – postage and handling <u>FREE</u>

    Total amount: _____

❏ Check ❏ Money Order

❏ VISA ❏ Master Card ❏ AMEX

Card Number_____Expiration date_____

Signature_____

If you would like your book(s) autographed, please indicate your name or the person's name(s) below:

_____

Send_____copy(ies) to:

Name _____

Address _____

City, State, Zip _____

Note: _____

Other books, tapes and products are available from New Paradigm Press. Write or call for information and prices.

ANNE PURYEAR

About the author:

Anne Puryear is a writer, therapist and ordained minister. She and her husband, psychologist and author Herbert Bruce Puryear, Ph.D., live in Scottsdale, Arizona. They are cofounders of the Logos Center, a non-denominational church, which includes a Holistic Health Division and an Educational Division. Their work is dedicated to understanding and healing the body, mind and spirit, developing spiritual leadership and teaching Practical Christian Mysticism.

Anne's work during the past twenty years has earned her wide recognition as a spiritual counselor, lecturer and modern day Christian Mystic. She and her husband have traveled and led tours all over the world. Her experiences and studies have made her a leading expert on teenage suicide and life after death. She is the author of *STEPHEN LIVES!: My Son Stephen: His Life, Suicide and Afterlife,* published by Simon and Schuster.